Aspects of Lucan

Four Historical Essays

by Linda Curran, Valerie Twomey,
Patricia Donohoe & Suzanne Pegley

Edited by Patricia Donohoe

LP
SV

First published in 2008
Published by LPSV Publishers

For more information, contact Suzanne Pegley,
'Blackwood', Mill Lane, Leixlip, Co. Kildare, Ireland

A catalogue record for this title is available
from the British Library

ISBN: 0-9541677-1-4

This book received support from the Heritage Council
under the 2008 Publications Grant Scheme, and also
from Fingal County Council.

This book was set in Bembo
Design and layout: www.thedrawingboard.ie
Printed in Ireland by Beta Print, Dublin

Aspects of Lucan

Four Historical Essays

TABLE *of* CONTENTS

Abbreviations

Lcn P. A. . . . . Lucan Parish Archives
NLI. . . . . National Library of Ireland
NAI. . . . . National Archives
RCB . . . . Representative Church Body
RCBL . . . . Representative Church Body Library
UCD . . . . University College Dublin
VMB . . . . Vestry Minute Book

Acknowledgments

There are a number of individuals we would like to thank with regard to the completion of this book. First of all we would like to acknowledge the continued help, support and understanding of our respective husbands; Frank, Brendan, Brian and Charlie.

Thanks are due to Dolores Collins, who willingly shared her unpublished thesis on the Shackleton's Mills with Linda. Also, to Lilian Harris of Lucan for providing a considerable amount of local knowledge and to Suzanne Pegley, for the use of her artwork.

Valerie expresses her gratitude to Donald Cromer, FRIAI, who shared with her his knowledge of the architectural heritage of St Andrew's Church and to Patricia Donohoe whose M.Litt. thesis proved an invaluable source of reference for her work. Also, to Brendan for his encouragement and debate during Valerie's research and for taking the photographs used in her essay.

Grateful thanks to Professor Jacqueline Hill (NUIM) who advised and encouraged Patricia during her initial research. To Mary Shackleton for access to the photographs of Jane Wigham Shackleton and to Brian for his photography of the parish records which appear in her essay.

Suzanne would like to express her thanks to two individuals for their invaluable contributions – Deborah Heller for generously sharing of her research, and Sir Charles Colthurst for his interest and support in her study of Lucan Demesne – she is most grateful. She would also like to to thank Christopher Moore for his continuing encouragement.

Finally we acknowledge the mutual support we received from each other since we began this journey.

List *of* Illustrations *and* Plates

The Manor of Lucan in Medieval Ireland

St. Andrew's Lucan – History, Architecture and Artworks

* Drawing of St Andrew's on page 34 courtesy D. Kenny

Protestant Philanthropy and Social Interaction

Lucan Demesne and the Liffey Valley

* Drawings and cartography by Suzanne Pegley

FOREWORD

Lucan, despite its long and vibrant history, has rarely been documented in print. There are several excellent publications by local authors in circulation. These provide Lucanians and visitors alike with a glimpse of what Lucan was like in the past and how it has developed in the present day.

Yet no major academic work has been released for over one hundred years.

Aspects of Lucan, like its title suggests, deals with specific areas of Lucan's history and heritage. It does not attempt to tell the whole story, but the topics it does deal with are covered comprehensively.

This work combines four distinctive essays on life at different stages of our village's history since medieval times. It provides a particular focus on the role played by the Protestant Ascendancy in its social and economic development up until recent times. It looks at many of the people, the places and architecture that made Lucan what it is today.

Aspects of Lucan is a valuable collection. It reminds us of our splendid historic and architectural heritage, of what we have already lost, of what still remains and what we must treasure and preserve for future generations.

Everyone needs a sense of place. This book will therefore be welcomed by those of us who are from Lucan, those who have lived in Lucan and those who can trace their roots back to the area. However it will also be of use to a much broader church, especially those with an interest in history, anthropology and architecture.

I would like to congratulate the authors for their dedication and attention to detail in putting *Aspects of Lucan* together and wish them every success with this important publication.

Paul Gogarty TD
Lucanian and member of Dáil Eireann

Preface

Lucan in the 1980s and early 1990s was simply a bottleneck to be endured on the road to somewhere much more interesting. But in the last fifteen years, Ireland has changed dramatically, experiencing the growth of a more vibrant economy and the beginning of immigration, rather than emigration. During this time, Lucan has developed from a village into a size that could now be described as a town. Indeed, with the construction of Adamstown, a second town is emerging in an area that was previously considered part of Lucan.

This book on the history of Lucan follows the successful *Aspects of Leixlip* produced in 2001 and, like the previous volume, consists of four essays covering different aspects of the history of Lucan. Three of these essays were especially researched with this publication in mind, while the fourth was prepared for an academic qualification.

Linda Curran presents a picture of Lucan in medieval Ireland, with particular emphasis on the Manor of Lucan in the thirteenth and fourteenth centuries. She also highlights some of the social and economic developments in the eighteenth and nineteenth centuries.

Valerie Twomey, in a similar vein to *Aspects of Leixlip*, looks at the architecture of the fine Church of Ireland building in the middle of the village. In collaboration with Donald Cromer, she has expanded the nucleus of his research into a fuller picture of the architectural development.

Patricia Donohoe, who has edited the publication, focuses in her essay on a core aspect from her Master's thesis. She examines the philanthropic contribution of the ascendancy and the significant role they played within the community of Lucan in the nineteenth century.

Suzanne Pegley writes on the history of Lucan House and Demesne in the context of the Liffey Valley. The house and parkland, so closely integrated into the town, are largely unknown to the new communities whose presence has substantially increased the population of Lucan.

Under the editorship of Mary Mulhall, the three publications *A History of Lucan*, *Lucan and Lucanians*, and most recently *Treasures of Lucan* have been extremely popular. Nevertheless, *Aspects of Lucan* represents the most significant academic study of Lucan since D'Alton's history of County Dublin was published in 1836.

By drawing on original research, this book seeks to update the history of Lucan for a modern audience and introduce material not previously covered. However, the history of Lucan is not complete with this publication, and it is hoped that other authors will open the historical horizons even wider.

"*In Claude's landscape all is lovely, all amiable, all is amenity and repose – the calm sunshine of the heart*" John Constable, 1836

The Manor *of* Lucan *in* Medieval Ireland

by Linda Curran

Introduction

This essay provides the reader with an overview of the settlement of Lucan, with a particular focus on the medieval period. There has been a settlement in this area since Early Christian times, and the site holds a place of strategic importance in Irish history. Lucan was on the edge of the *Dylinarskiri*, the area of Viking control around Dublin which extended from Arklow to the river Delvin above Skerries, and along the river Liffey to the Salmon Leap at Leixlip.

The Vikings passed by Lucan in 917 AD on their journey west, and settled at Cooldrinagh, near Leixlip. It is not known if they settled in Lucan, but developments of the two areas have been remarkably similar over the years, and it is quite possible that the Vikings also took advantage of the strategic site in Lucan overlooking the river.

The Norman invasion of 1169 AD made a significant impact on Lucan, and the area was under the control of Anglo Norman lords from that time onwards. Under the feudal system the English crown had the power to grant land to nobles, and the manorial system of landholding was gradually imposed on their newly conquered territory.[1] Successive Kings made grants of land to the church and to Norman lords, who in turn sub-divided the lands while keeping a large portion for their own use. The first of these grants was made to Alard Fitz William by Henry II, who created the manor of Lucan.

The manor remained in Anglo-Norman hands for almost two hundred years, and it is noteworthy that it remained within one family, the de Peche family, for almost half of that time. Developments in Lucan during this time closely mirrored those of Leixlip, with in some cases shared ownership of major lands in both towns as a result of grants by the reigning monarch.

The manor of Lucan, later known as Lucan Castle, was the most significant structure in the area, but a number of other castles were built in the area for fortification, and later residential use. These included Ballyowen Castle, Ballydowd Castle, Fyanstown Castle and Adamstown Castle. The building of stone castles in Lucan and nearby Leixlip is an indication of the importance of these sites to the Anglo-Normans as lesser settlements had earthwork structures which were much quicker to erect.

It is also interesting that Lucan fitted the pattern for Norman settlements, as it had a number of the desirable locational attributes which were attractive to those colonizing the country. These included pre-Norman monastic sites, river crossings, navigable rivers and coastal sites, and we can see that at least two of these factors were present in Lucan.

The original church in Lucan, the Church of the Blessed Virgin, is believed to date from the early thirteenth century. Its name gives us an indication that this church may have existed before the arrival of the Normans, as it was a Norse custom to dedicate a church to the Virgin Mary when using the name of a female saint. There were also a number of other churches in the areas adjoining Lucan. Of particular note was nearby Esker, which in medieval times was known as Esker of the Seven Churches. In more recent times, the village of Lucan was almost unique in Ireland in the nineteenth century when churches were built by four different Christian denominations to meet the needs of their parishioners. These churches exist side by side in Lucan to the present day.

The rise of the Irish nobility and their growing political importance is evident in the granting of the manors of Lucan, Kildrought and Kilmacrydock by King Richard II to the Fitzgerald family, the Earls of Kildare, in the late fourteenth century. The Fitzgeralds had control of these lands until they were confiscated in the mid-sixteenth century, and developments in Lucan at this time mirrored major events in Ireland. The arrival of Oliver Cromwell in 1649, the establishment of the Commonwealth and the restoration of the monarchy in 1660, affected key families in the area, first by confiscation of their lands and second, the restoration of these lands on petition to King Charles II.

Originally a village dependent on agriculture for the creation of limited employment, from the mid seventeenth century Lucan saw the establishment of a number of industries dependent on a good supply of flowing water from the river Liffey. These included corn, flour and woollen mills, iron works and a linen printing house. During the seventeenth and eighteenth centuries, these enterprises flourished in tandem with industry in the rest of the country, but a period of decline began after the 1801 Act of Union, when increased competition from Britain and the industrialisation of Ulster seriously damaged the ability of their counterparts in the south of Ireland to continue to trade.

It is remarkable to think that for a considerable period of time from the late eighteenth to the early twentieth century, Lucan was a place for the citizens of Dublin to visit and enjoy. The village provided a pleasant day trip and a change of scenery. A visit to the seaside, which we today take for granted, was at that time regarded as more appropriate for invalids, or those recovering from illness. People placed greater emphasis on travelling along the Strawberry Beds to Lucan, and on to the Salmon Leap in Leixlip, to enjoy the country air and the attractive scenery.

The beauty of the Liffey Valley has been noted in many travelogues over the years, and the area around Lucan was part of a created landscape which flowed from the Phoenix Park along the Strawberry Beds to Lucan, and followed the river Liffey as far as Straffan. The intention at the time was to imitate the Italian countryside, then seen as an indicator of sophisticated enlightenment.

The number of visitors greatly increased in the nineteenth century when first one, and then a second, sulphur spring was discovered. Improvements in transport assisted in this development, and travel by coach, by horseback and on foot gradually changed to journeys by steam train and then by tram. A hotel was built, the original Spa Hotel which was later replaced by the building we know today, and accommodation was provided for the larger numbers of people travelling to Lucan to take the waters and to attend concerts and balls. But, as with every fashion, other opportunities for leisure became available to the general population, and visitors to Lucan gradually declined in the early twentieth century.

From that time on, however, the population of Lucan itself began to increase, and this situation accelerated from the 1980s onwards. Since then, Lucan and the surrounding areas have experienced very rapid development, and this has been mirrored in many other villages in county Dublin. The transformation of former green sites to provide houses and related facilities has once again attracted people to move out to this suburb of Dublin, and Lucan is now a commuter village with residents travelling to the city centre to work. It is striking to note that once again there is growing diversity in population, as newcomers to Ireland settle in the area and make Lucan their home. It would therefore appear that Lucan has come full circle from the arrival of the Normans and possibly the Vikings before them, almost one thousand years ago.

Following this initial exploration of the development of the village of Lucan, we will now look at the history of Lucan and its place in Medieval Ireland.

LUCAN IN MEDIEVAL IRELAND

> "The eastern triangle is the geographical nucleus from which men have seen their best chance of commanding the whole country. And yet the same district is also one of the most vulnerable parts of Ireland, the longest break in its defence of mountain ring, with the estuaries of the Liffey and the Boyne to beckon the invader onwards".[2]

The name *Leamhcán* means "Place of Elms". It is a derivative of the word leamh, or leamhán, which means elm-tree, and which we can assume referred to the presence of a significant wooded area.[3] There has been a settlement at Lucan since Early Christian times, and the village of Lucan held a place of strategic importance in Irish history. It was situated at one of the key crossing points of the river Liffey, and the first bridge across the river was built before 1216, in the reign of King John. There are many references to the village of Lucan in historical documents, and manuscripts from medieval times contain a number of versions of its name.

Composite map showing the principal Slighe routes 123 AD

Figure 1: Slighe Roads

Variously called Liuecan, Lyuecan, Lyuechan, and Lyuekan, these give an indication of the Anglicisation of the area's original name.

Lucan was also significant for its location on the Slighe-Mor, or Eiscir-Riada, the ancient road from Dublin to Galway.[4] In early times, roads connected the main centres of life in Ireland. There were five great highways which had, since Conn Ced-cathach (c.200 AD) stretched out on every side from Tara.[5] These roads are known today as the Slighe system. They were Slighe-Asail, Slighe-Miodhluachra, Slighe-

Cualann, Slighe-Dala and Slighe-Mor. Nearby Eiscir, or Esker, is also the name of the ridge of sand hills which ran from Dublin to Galway, and which was the boundary between the north and south of Ireland in the second century, most noteworthy for its connection with Eoghan Mor and Conn of One Hundred Battles.[6] The Slighe system was still in use in Ireland during Norse rule, and when the Anglo-Normans came to Ireland they found 'many highways available for their campaigns'.[7]

By the tenth century, the Vikings had captured strongholds in Waterford, Limerick, Cork and Wexford. They used navigable rivers on their journey inland, and during the Viking era the river Liffey was known as Life-na-Longa, or the Liffey of the Ships, because of the number of masts to be seen on the river.[8] In 917 AD the Vikings sailed up the river Liffey as far as Leixlip, but were unable to travel any further because of the impassable Salmon Leap. It is quite possible that the Vikings may have settled on the strategic site in Lucan overlooking the river.

Two centuries later, by 1169, the Normans had arrived in Ireland and successfully captured Dublin, which had been the capital of the Viking kingdom for almost three centuries. The Early Christian settlement at Lucan was one of those in County Dublin taken over by the newly arrived Anglo-Norman lords. The early establishment of a territorial framework, allied with the likelihood that the most desirable sites within them would be used for settlements established by seignorial lords or principal grantees, indicates the probability of such settlements possessing significant locational advantages, particularly for urban developments.[9] It is evident that Lucan fits the pattern for

Figure 2: The origins and development of villages in County Dublin

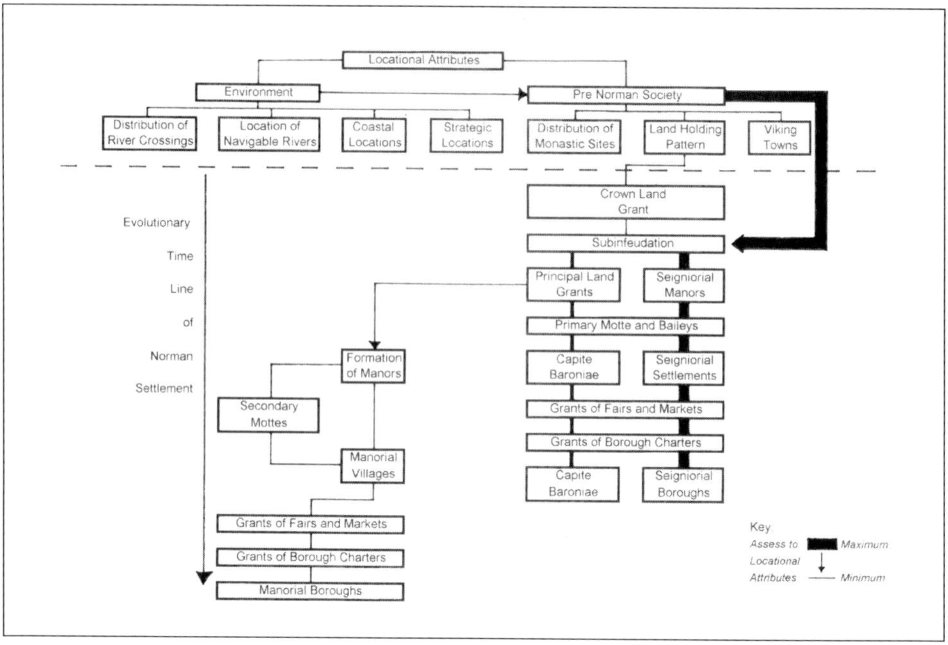

Figure 3: Model of medieval urban evolution

Norman settlements, particularly due to its strategic location, its infrastructure and its pre-existing settlement.[10]

The newcomers favoured sites which were either beside or close to rivers, so that they were well supplied with water. They also preferred places which had an existing infrastructure, and particularly chose sites which were adequately connected by road, and had some political significance. The majority of these conditions were found in Lucan, with its strategic site beside the river Liffey and on the Slighe Mhor, and they also created the conditions for an Anglo-Norman presence in nearby Leixlip.

Once they arrived in Ireland, the Anglo-Normans secured their lands by building castles, which functioned first as advanced strong points in hostile country, and then as centres of control.[11] The most important feature of this strategy was that the medieval castles protected the territory by virtue of their location, and their closeness to one another. "The very existence of an encastellated frontier landscape – 'one of the first systematically fortified frontiers in Europe' – tells us less about the threat of the Irish to the colony than it does about the Norman perceptions".[12]

During the Norman conquest of Ireland, there was a marked degree of direct continuity from the pre-existing societal and settlement systems.[13] The Norman settlement of Ireland was carried out by the Crown through the allocation of lordships to several major grantees, and this process was particularly characteristic of eastern Leinster. The magnates then sub-divided their grants among tenants, keeping large areas for themselves.[14] This is clearly seen in the settlement of Lucan through grants from the reigning monarch, and the process can also be observed in the neighbouring towns of Leixlip and Celbridge.

Henry II visited Ireland in 1171, staying for seven months, and during that time he established a feudal system of government for the country. Under the feudal system of tenure, all lands were surrendered to the king upon the death of the tenant. Lands also reverted to the Crown if the tenant had no heirs, or if the heir was not of age. Most nobles paid homage to the King, when he held court in Dublin and other important locations.

We know much of this time through the Calendar of Ormond Deeds, more commonly called the Ormond Deeds, which includes a record of documents from the year 1180 to the reign of Elizabeth I. These Deeds "contains abundant evidence for the medley of races and languages, French, Flemish, Welsh, Gaelic, Norse and Saxon which obtained in medieval Ireland".[15] An address by Prince John, c.1185, gives us an indication of this diversity, when he commences with "John, son of the King of England, and lord of Ireland, to all his men, French, English and Irish, greetings".[16] John visited Ireland as King in 1210, towards the end of his reign, in an attempt to set up a permanent government structure based on English lines. He succeeded in establishing an Exchequer, and a Chancery, but it was not until 1297 in the reign of Edward I that the first Irish Parliament was summoned.

"The new foreign aristocracy were generous patrons of monks and canons".[17] Warrisus (Werris) de Peche, who had been granted the manor of Lucan by Henry II before 1203, founded a priory on land between Lucan and Leixlip, which was dedicated to St Katherine in 1219 and occupied by the canons regular of St Victor. The Church of the Blessed Virgin Mary, situated in Lucan Demesne, was the original church of Lucan, and in 1220 de Peche granted 'the church of the Blessed Virgin of Lucan to the Priory of St Katherine'.[18] It is most likely that this church existed prior to the arrival of

Table 1:
Kings and Queens of England

Henry II	1154-1189
Richard I	1189-1199
John	1199-1216
Henry III	1216-1272
Edward I	1272-1307
Edward II	1307-1327
Edward III	1327-1377
Richard II	1377-1399
Henry IV	1399-1413
Henry V	1413-1422
Edward IV	1461-1483
Richard III	1483-1485
Henry VII	1485-1509
Henry VIII	1509-1547
Edward VI	1547-1553
Mary I	1553-1558
Elizabeth I	1558-1603
James I	1603-1625
Charles I	1625-1649
Commonwealth	1649-1660
Charles II	1660-1685

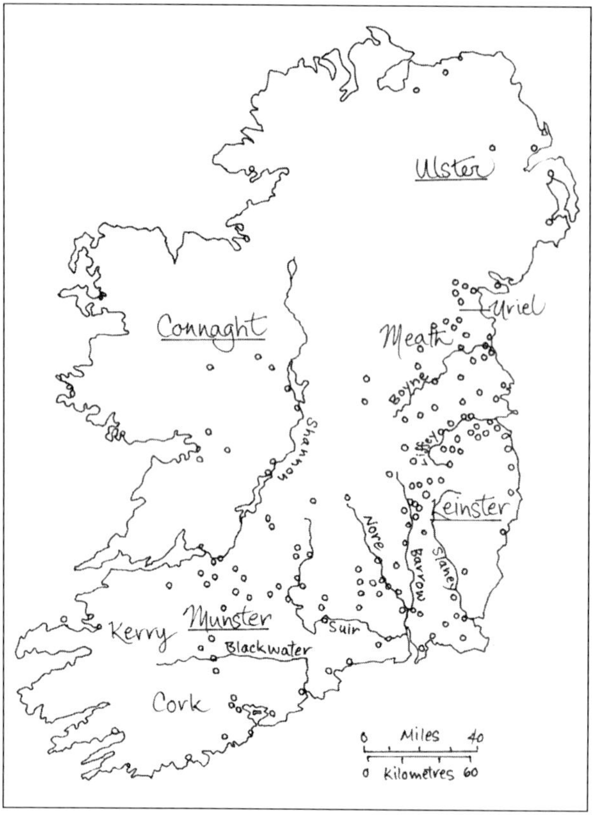

Figure 4: Ireland: distribution of boroughs

the Normans, because of the Norse custom, after they converted to Christianity, of always dedicating a church to the Virgin Mary when using the name of a female saint. This 'cult of St Mary' was particularly notable in pre-Norman Ireland of the twelfth century.[19]

The Anglo-Normans successfully introduced the manorial system of landholding in their newly conquered territory.[20] As we have seen, land was granted to the nobles, and also to archbishops and monasteries. But land was also retained by the Crown, including the royal manors of Esker and Newcastle.

The Anglo-Norman settlement at Lucan included the manor house, the parish church and a number of cottages. This became the manorial centre, where all aspects of daily life were carried out. Tenants brought their rents, paid their tithes and also occasionally attended the manorial court.[21] Lucan was one of the medieval settlements where tenants held their land by burgage tenure,[22] and as a result they enjoyed greater autonomy.

The fourteenth century was a time of considerable unrest in Ireland, particularly during the Bruce invasion of 1315-1317. In 1315 a commission was given to Warin Oweyn and Walter Fox to elect eighty men in Newcastle, Lucan and Esker to maintain nightly watch there with six other men-at-arms, with mailed horses, against the King's enemies of the Leinster mountains in Tassagard.[23] Shortly afterwards, in 1317, the forces of Edward and Robert Bruce camped in nearby Leixlip on their march from Castleknock to Naas. By 1326, the situation of the manors in the estate of the see of Dublin was described as being divided into two groups, with the manors south of Dublin forming a chain which skirted the Dublin mountains. These manors were exposed to continual incursions by the mountaineers.[24]

Edward II, and his successor Edward III, created five earldoms in Ireland in an effort to strengthen control of the country. The first of these was the earldom of Ulster, and some years later John Fitz Thomas Fitzgerald was created earl of Kildare in 1316.[25] The Fitzgerald family played a vital role in controlling Ireland on behalf of the Crown for more than one hundred years, and the influential post of Lord Deputy was most often held by the Earl of Kildare. But by 1435 royal authority in Ireland had been reduced to an small area surrounding Dublin, and a report to the king stated that 'his writ was confined to an area thirty miles long and twenty miles wide in counties Dublin, Meath, Louth and Kildare'.[26] This area gradually became known as the Pale. The earliest known use of this term was in 1446-7, when the Irish leader Aodh Ruadh Mac Mathghamhna promised 'to carrie nothing oute of the inglishe pale contrarie to the statutes'.[27]

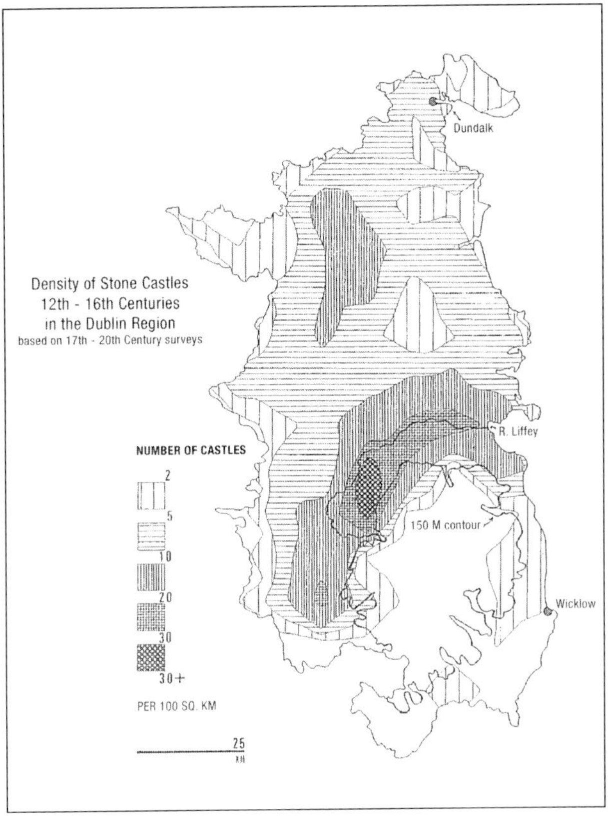

Figure 5: Density of stone castles (twelfth to sixteenth centuries) in the Dublin region (based on seventeenth and twentieth-century surveys)

The area under effective control of the Dublin administration therefore contracted significantly during the first half of the fifteenth century, and some historians have said that this was due to the inability to put sufficient forces in the field for long enough to achieve any lasting expansion or stabilisation of the frontier.[28] An example of the type of action which was taken at the time was in 1455, when orders were issued for the building of barriers and towers on the bridges of Lucan and Kilmainham, and beside the wall of St Mary's Abbey, to repel the 'Irish enemies' and 'English rebels' who enter into Fingal by night and there kill, rob and destroy the liege people of the King.[29]

The medieval period of Irish history lasted from 1169 until c1650, with the 'impetus of the Cromwellian re-conquest initiating widespread landscape alterations'.[30] Following the execution of James I, and royalist support in Ireland, Oliver Cromwell was sent to Ireland as Lord Lieutenant and Commander in Chief to bring the country under control. By 1653, confiscation of property was being undertaken on a wide scale, and by 1658 two-thirds of all Irish land was either owned or occupied by English settlers. The population of many areas was also affected, and Lucan suffered a twenty eight per cent decline in its population between 1650 and 1660, due in great measure to the confiscation of the land from the Sarsfield family.[31] Following the Restoration, in 1660, King Charles II made efforts to redress the injustices done, and much land was restored on petition.

"After the great land transfers from catholic into protestant hands which followed the cromwellian conquest, the manorial system was replaced by a commercial tenant-landlord relationship".[32] Where a landlord held an estate, or where a confiscated estate was not broken up, villages were kept intact and sometimes even enlarged. By the nineteenth century, there were eight villages in County Dublin 'which seem to have been influenced by the estate system'. Four of these, including Lucan, were medieval manorial sites and four others were post-cromwellian.[33]

As we have seen in this section, the settlement of Lucan by the Anglo-Normans in the medieval period brought the area under the control of the English crown, and land was granted to a succession of nobles in order to retain support for the King. We will now look in more detail at the manor of Lucan, the most significant of the lands granted by the King under the feudal system.

THE MANOR OF LUCAN

> "Here there is a very faire house, a chapel, some thatch houses and Cabbins, and a good Stone bridge crossing the river Liffey".[34]

The manor of Lucan was created in 1169, when Henry II made the first grant of land to Alard Fitz William. Alard, son of William, chamberlain to the King, was the first feoffee[35] of the manor of Leuekan and of all other lands later named in the charters in Ireland for donation by King John, then lord of Ireland. These lands were to be held by free service of six pairs of furred gloves of lambskin, and a thabur (tunic) yearly in Michaelmas term.[36] Alard's daughter, Cicely de Langetot, was his heir, and her marriage to Sir Baldwin de Coudrei produced a son, Fouke de Coudrei. The Ormond Deeds later noted that their grandson, Sir Pires de Coudrei 'now demands the land'.[37]

By 1203 the manor of Lucan had been granted to Werris (Werrick) de Peche, who was created Lord of Lucan. James Mills[38] tells us that Lieucon was given to Wyrrys (Werrick) de Peche or Pecchie of Hampshire, who paid 40 marks and a palfrey[39] for the confirmation of the land, and this grant was confirmed by King John on condition that this payment was made to the King's Treasurer. A small castle was built on the land, originally a tall square tower, and the building was then added to over the years, and described as 'battlemented and irregular'. By the thirteenth century, the lands at Lucan were said to contain a manorial residence with a large curtilage[40] and garden, a mill and a dovecote. By this time a village of some size had grown up around the manor, with perhaps two or three dozen houses.

This is in keeping with the manorial village of the time, which is described as a nucleated settlement containing a church and generally, but not necessarily, a castle, with the population primarily involved in agriculture and supportive local industry, such as milling.[41] "Monopolising the best land in the county, manorial villages provided a widespread and enduring settlement network in which there was little room left for initiation of newer settlements".[42]

Links between the noble families in Lucan and Leixlip were very strong, and ownership of lands in both villages by the same family was not uncommon. For example, Werris de Peche married the granddaughter of Adam de Hereford, one of the favourites of Richard de Clare (also known as Strongbow), who had been granted the lands in the neighbouring village of Leixlip. Their daughter Alice married Radulf FitzNicholas, (also known as Ralph Pippard or Pypard), and their son, Radulf Pipard, born 1267, came into possession of the lands in Leixlip by service of 2½ knights fees to William de Vescy, lord of Kildare. This was the custom at the time, later replaced by monetary payments rather than personal service.[43]

Ownership of the manor of Lucan passed from the first Werris de Peche to his son Werris, and then to his grandson William de Peche who died before 1270. Under the feudal system of tenure,[44] all lands were surrendered to the king upon the death of a tenant, and for a short time after William's death, the lands at Lucan reverted to the Crown, as his son Henry was a minor. An account of the manor of Lucan for 1274, when it was in the hands of an escheator[45] on behalf of

Table 2: Accounts of the manor of Lucan, 1274 from the Pipe Roll for 2 Ed. I

Rent Paid	Receipts
Rent of betaghs	67s 0d
Corn of demesne lands	50s 0d
Rent of farmers	7s 5½d
Rent of free tenants	6s 0d
Rent of burgages	23s 6½d
Receipts of mill	17s 9½d
Profits of court	3s 4d
Meadow	0s 18d
Pasturage	0s 10d
Prise of Ale	0s 2d
Profits of garden	3s 4d
Profits of dove cote	0s 6d
Curtilage	0s 4d

Note: During this period it was noted that the betaghs paid 67 shillings for their rent, and were only paid 9s. 4d. for their work.

the King, shows rents similar to those obtained from Church lands. Table 2 details receipts related to a period of four and a half months in 1273, when the total received was £9.11s.10d:[46]

This estate was typical of its neighbours, and that of the native agricultural population who continued to occupy the greater part of the land after the Norman settlement, yielding to their Norman lords services which took the place of those formerly exacted by the Irish chief. The grantees of the land were in effect new proprietors of land which was already settled, and whose tenants then continued on the land much as before.[47]

When Henry de Peche came of age in 1285 he took possession of the manor, and gave as rent to the Crown a thabur (tunic) and four pairs of furred gloves. When he died in 1291, his daughter Roesia was placed under the guardianship of Robert Hanstede and his wife of Chester. Some time later, Roesia married the son of her guardian, John Hanstede, and they subsequently came into possession of the lands.

In 1305 the Hanstedes became involved in a law suit with Ralph Pipard of Leixlip and the King over the salmon fisheries on the river Liffey. The decision was made that half the fisheries belonged to Leixlip, and the Sheriff was directed to remove a weir which had recently been erected at Lucan which had 'much narrowed the Liffey'. There was much further litigation around this time, particularly in relation to Robert de Nottingham, who was a very wealthy member of the Norman aristocracy and Lord Mayor of Dublin, and who succeeded the Hanstedes in Lucan in 1315.

For example, in April of that year a royal licence was given to John de Hanstede to enfeoff Robert de Notyngham in the manor of Lyuecan,[48] the property being held of the King in capite.[49] One month later, in May 1315, in the reign of Edward II, the following deed gives an indication of the size and wealth of the estate:

> John de Hanstede grants, releases and quit claims[50] to Robert de Notingham and his heirs and assigns all claims to the water mill at Lotereleston in county Dublin and in the manor of Lucan with all its appurtenances viz messuages,[51] lands, meadows, woods, passes, quarries, marl-pits, sand-pits, rabbit warrens, homages, rents, services, customs of burgesses, farmers, cottagers and betaghs, both English and Irish etc to have and to hold of the chief lords of those fees by the services thereto pertaining.[52]

In May 1315, the Ormond Deeds note a letter in French from John de Hanstede to the Prior of St John of Jerusalem, confirming that he had granted the manor of Lucan to Robert de Notyngham. Also in May 1315, the Ormond Deeds refer to an Indenture with regard to the manor of Lyuecan, and it would appear that Robert de Notingham owed 2,000 marks to John De Hanstede. This would have been a considerable debt at the time, and the Indenture refers to a settlement of one-third part of the manor of Lyuecan. It is noted that Eleanor, formerly wife of Henry de Peche, held one-third in dowry, and also a third part of two parts of the manor was held by Robert de Wileby and his wife Alicia, through a dowry to Alicia.

The term of the settlement was twenty four years, and many conditions are listed, including taking into account a situation where any part of the manor should fall into the hands of the King. The most significant reason for this was when the tenant died, and his heir was not of age. The lands would then revert to the crown until the heir reached his majority. In this settlement, if all proceeded in accordance with the agreement, Robert de Notyngham's debt was to be exonerated at the end of the term.[53]

The legal difficulties in relation to the manor continued in 1316, and in April of that year

> David Styward granted to Robert de Notynghame, citizen of Dublin, one burgage, viz a messuage with curtilages, in the town of Lyuechan that lies between the burgage formerly belonged to William Styward and Robert de Notton, stretching in length from the high street (regia strata) of the said town to the water of Aven Lyffe, to have and to hold to him and his heirs for ever.[54]

In 1318, a deed by Robert de Notyngham appointed Richard Resoun his attorney for placing Sir John Barby in seisin[55] of the manor of Lucan. Robert de Notyngham died in 1327, and his son William also died shortly afterwards. At the time of William's death, he was described as having 'much livestock, including a thousand sheep and two hundred lambs, and a house well furnished with plate and beds of linen and wool'.

In December 1339, the Ormond Deeds record a quit claim by Thomas Colchestre to John de Bath and his wife Eglentina of lands in Dublin, Merrion and Lucan. It was not until February 1341, fifteen months later, that an agreement entitled a "final concord" was reached between Simon Fitz Richard (plaintiff) and John de Bath and Eglentina his wife on the manor of Lucan and a mill at Lutereleston. John and Eglentina agreed the manor to be the proper right of Simon, and they released and quit claimed to Simon and his heirs for ever. In return Simon gave John and Eglentina de Bath a sparrow hawk.

In 1386, King Richard II enfeoffed Maurice, fourth Earl of Kildare, in the manors of Lucan, Kildrought and Kilmacrydock, to hold for ever, in capite. However, the land vacilitated within the King's gift, and in 1395 two parts of the manor and water mill was committed to chaplain John Route. It was further noted in 1409 that two parts of the manor of Lucan were granted to chaplain Thomas Hunt and to Walter

Hern. In 1416 Henry V similarly granted the whole of the manor, with Kildrought and Kilmacrydock, to John, son of Sir John Talbot, at the service of two knights.[56]

As confirmation of the Fitzgerald family's standing with the crown, Gerald, eighth earl of Kildare, received the manor and lordship of Leixlip on the occasion of his marriage in 1496. Elizabeth Fitzgerald, wife of Garret, ninth Earl of Kildare, died at Lucan and is buried in the graveyard beside Lucan Demesne. The Fitzgerald family retained possession of their lands until 1536, when the lands in Lucan and Leixlip were confiscated by Henry VIII following the Silken Thomas revolt. It was said at the time that "the blood of the Geraldines is corrupted towards the crown of England".[57]

In 1554 the lands at Lucan came into the possession of Matthew King. In a communication from the Queen to the Lord Deputy and the Lord Chancellor,[58] it was stated that

> "Whereas, our well-beloved servant, Mathew Kinge, now presently holdeth of us in farm our manor of Lucane, in the county of Dublin, the years whereof are near expired; in consideration of his long and honest service, our pleasure is, that you shall take a surrender of his old lease, and make a sufficient lease again to him and his assigns in writing, under our great seal, for twenty-one years; paying unto us and our successors in our Exchequer the yearly accustomed rent due for the same, with such other covenants and conditions as are mentioned in his former lease." Westminster, December 13, 1553.

Subsequently the lands came into the possession of Sir Theophilus Jones, initially a supporter of the commonwealth but who later placed his allegiance with the restoration. This period, and that of the Sarsfield family's possession of Lucan Castle, is dealt with in greater detail in another section of this book.

LUCAN AS A FASHIONABLE RESORT

> "The sweet choristers of the air, the solemn tones of church bells, the loud sounding horn of the factory, rousing the weaver from his calm sleep to the busy loom, the pleasure-seekers, with song and laugh and instrumental music, revelling in this lap of Nature, give to Lucan a distinct and local splendour"[59]

Lucan in the eighteenth century was a small country village, with some well-developed industry, surrounded by prosperous agricultural lands. A drawing by Joseph Fisher showed a 'pastoral landscape incorporating the created landscapes that were becoming so popular at the time', and which was particularly well

Plate 1: Lucan Castle

demonstrated within the Liffey Valley. This landscape was the ideal of the time, and it flowed from the Phoenix Park and along the Strawberry Beds to Lucan and on to Celbridge. The landscape was intended to mimic the Italian countryside, which was very important as an indicator of sophisticated enlightenment.[60]

Lucan was very attractive to the citizens of Dublin and many tourists were drawn to the area. It has been included in a number of travelogues, the earliest of which was Dr John D'Alton's *History of County Dublin* (1838). Many books and journals over the years have described Lucan in almost lyrical terms, due to its situation and the countryside surrounding the village. Lucan was a place of fashionable resort and pleasant occasional residence, with beautifully diversified scenery.[61] The surrounding land was highly cultivated, with fertile soil and abundant crops, and he noted boats passing along the river Liffey laden with fish and with timber.

Lewis' Topographical Dictionary (1837) provides a good description of Lucan in the early nineteenth century, as a post-town and parish on the mail road to Galway

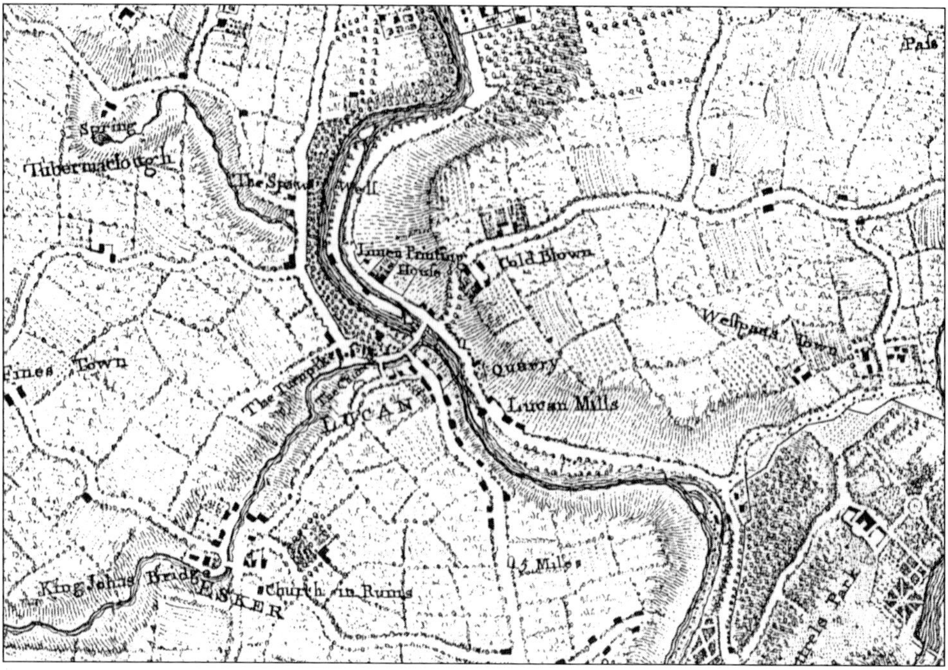

Plate 2: Rocque's Map of Lucan (1762)

and Sligo. There were 1,755 inhabitants in the Lucan area at the time, of which 1,229 lived in the village itself. According to Lewis, Lucan was "beautifully situated in a fertile vale on the eastern bank of the river Liffey". There was a handsome stone bridge with one arch, built in 1794, and ornamented with balustrades of cast iron.

On the other side of the bridge was a picturesque glebe with an incumbent, Rev. H. E. Price. The town contained 187 houses, most of which were well built, and many were used for lodgings for the visitors who came to take the waters. These waters were found to be "efficacious on scarbatic, bilious and rheumatic affectations".[62]

D'Alton (1838) further describes the locality as being "so sweetly situated at the junction of the little river Griffin with the Liffey, and once much and deservedly frequented on account of the beauty of its scenery, the salubrity of its air, and the vicinity of medicinal springs of experienced efficacy". However, the "fickleness of fashion, the want of encouragement from the proprietor, the unwelcome presence of turnpikes, the diversion of the great western line of road and the removal of the cotton factory have, however, consigned Lucan to unmerited obscurity".[63]

"The sheltered cot, the cultivated form,
The never-failing brook, the busy mill,
The decent church that topt the neighbouring hill"[64]

According to Donegan (1902), the Wicklow and Dublin mountains formed 'a glorious and majestic' background, with an enhancing view of the river Liffey, its well wooded slopes on one side and the prolific Strawberry Beds on the other. In county Dublin there was not a fairer spot than Lucan and its surroundings – *"Here nature does a house for one erect, - Nature! The fairest architect"*.

The discovery of two sulphur springs helped to make the area attractive to tourists. The first sulphur spring was discovered at Chapel Hill early in the 18th century and became very popular with citizens of Dublin. Every weekend, many travelled out by coach, on horseback and by foot to take the waters and to seek cures for a range of ailments such as skin diseases and rheumatism. Health and leisure resorts also developed throughout Britain in the early eighteenth century, for the social elites, in places such as Bath, Tunbridge Wells and Leamington.[65]

The original spa was gradually abandoned in favour of a second sulphur spring, known as the Boiling Spring because of its temperature, which was discovered in 1758 on the banks of the river Liffey, one mile outside Lucan on the road to Leixlip.

By 1789 Lucan was "the favourite summer resort, and the well was crowded with persons of condition who often formed dancing parties at a ballroom which had been built before that time". But it was not always such pleasant events which were noted, and in 1787 an incident at the Lucan races led to rioting. The magistrate was forced to intervene, and the High Sheriff went out to Lucan with a strong guard, struck the tents and ended the event.[66]

In order to accommodate visitors to the spring, a handsome Spa House was built, with a central building and two wings providing accommodation for families. The Spa House contained an Assembly Room which was sixty two feet long and twenty two feet wide, used regularly for concerts and balls. In 1795 the ballroom was converted

Plate 3: Spa House, Lucan, Co Dublin

into the building we know now as the County Bar. Behind the County Bar stands the Crescent, a terrace of Georgian houses which was originally used to provide accommodation for the visitors who came to take the waters, and later became a school for boys. Houses in the Crescent are now in private ownership.

D'Alton referred to the Lucan Spa House as a "well kept and once a well frequented hotel, whence a tunnel under the road leads to the spa, which rises close to the river Liffey, and is impregnated as strongly, perhaps, as any other natural spring with carbonate of lime and sulphurated nitrogen gas. The water, though limpid, emits a peculiarly offensive odour, and the taste is equally disagreeable. It is but fifteen feet deep, contains about eighty gallons of water, and when emptied fills again in an hour".[67] An analysis of the spring in 1822 identified carbonates of soda, lime, magnesia, silex, miriate soda and sulphur sulphate.

The discovery of two spas in the area, together with improved transport from Dublin city, gave Lucan a new lease of life and for a considerable time Lucan was a very popular destination for a day trip from the city. The spa became famous for its medicinal qualities and Dr Rutty lists more than fifty cases of various diseases which were observed as being cured by taking the waters. A gentleman at the end of the eighteenth century who was confined to his room counted the people who passed his window on their way to visit the spa, and this remarkable record provides us with some idea of the popularity of the spa:[68]

55 coaches	29 post-chaises
25 noddies	82 jaunting cars
20 gigs	6 open landaus
221 common cars	450 horsemen

Citizens of Dublin travelled in the evenings and at weekends to take the waters, and to attend concerts and dances. For an indication of the scale of some events, the *Freeman's Journal* (September 1811) reported on a ball and supper which took place in Lucan, "brilliantly attended by 110 of the first rank and consequence in the kingdom". Those attending sat down to supper at 1 am, and the ball ended at 6 am.

Lucan benefitted largely from the nineteenth century view that the seaside was a health resort for invalids, and for those recovering from illness. The majority of people preferred a visit to the country, and Lucan was particularly well situated for a day trip. The journey along the Liffey Valley, through the Strawberry Beds to Lucan and then on to the Salmon Leap at Leixlip, was more fashionable and more attractive to the citizens of Dublin at that time.

The short distance from the metropolis also rendered the town 'a place of fashionable resort and of pleasant occasional residence'. The increase in tourism, together with the prosperous farms nearby and the establishment of a number of

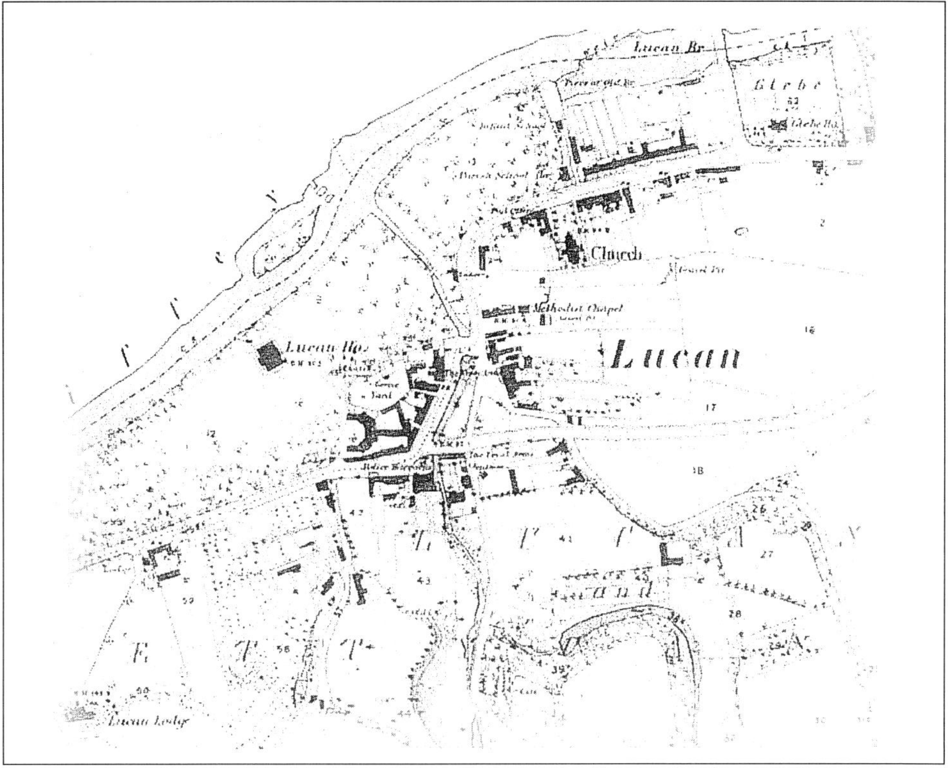

Plate 4: Ordnance Survey Map (1864)

industries, led to the creation of employment and a rising prosperity in the area.[69]

Lucan was 'galvanized' into life again by the construction of the tramway. There were now three ways to travel to Lucan, by tram, by Great Southern railway and by Midlands railway. On Sundays bands performed in the village, and it became "a well attended and fashionable promenade".[70] In 1908 Lucan was described by Charles J. Davey as 'the loveliest spot in county Dublin'. The tram went right into the centre of Lucan, and also ran more frequently than the railways.

The village of Lucan today is relatively unchanged from the way it looked in the 1800s, and the terrace of Georgian houses has been maintained in good condition. The area is now one of the fastest growing suburban areas of Ireland. No longer somewhere to visit for a day out, Lucan is increasingly seen as a desirable place to live and has become part of the urban growth of Dublin city.

The availability of land surrounding the village has meant the creation of large areas of residential accommodation stretching as far as the Royal canal, and this has

Plate 5: The Anna Liffey Mill, Lucan, County Dublin

led to a dramatic increase in population in the past ten years alone. But many links to the past remain. New housing developments created since the 1970s have been given names such as Earlsfort, Rochfort, Ballyowen, Ballydowd, Finnstown and Adamstown. Other local names of interest include Hanbury Lane,[71] Chapel Hill,[72] Watery Lane[73] and Tinker's Hill.[74] Despite this continued development, and the fact that it is sometimes considered to be a commuter town for Dublin, Lucan has managed to retain the character and charm which made it such a desirable destination in the eighteenth and nineteenth centuries.

We have seen in this section how Lucan benefited from its setting by the river Liffey as a means of attracting visitors to take the waters and enjoy the beautiful scenery. The river also provided the means to sustain industry and this, together with developments in transport, will be examined next.

INDUSTRIAL HERITAGE

There is evidence of economic and industrial activity in Lucan for almost one thousand years, dating back to the Anglo Norman settlement of the area. As described previously, the manorial village was the centre of economic life, and all activities associated with daily life were carried out there. Mills were an essential element of Anglo-Norman settlements, and tenants of the manor were legally bound to grind their corn in the lord's mill.[75] In medieval times the Pale contained two milling regions, in the Boyne Valley and the Liffey Valley,[76] and a number of mills were established along the north bank of the river.

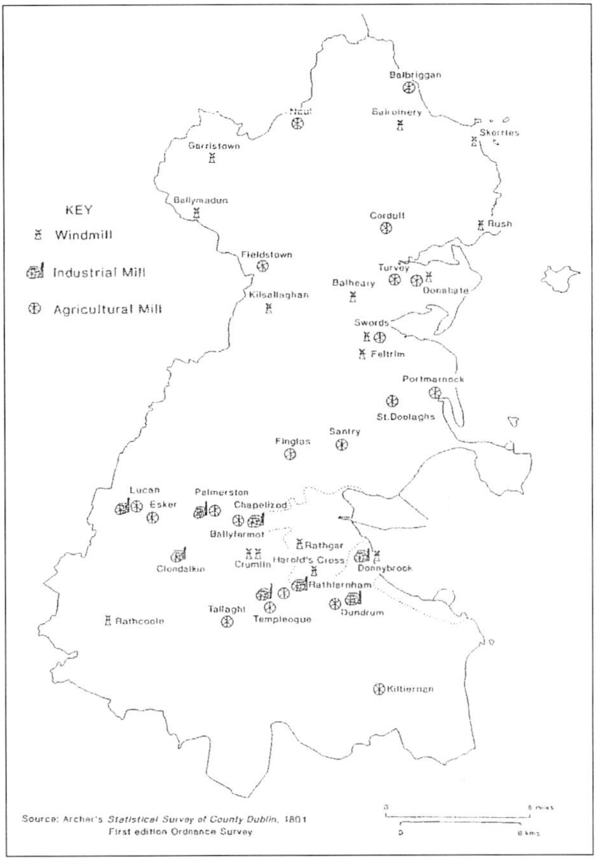

Figure 6: Mills in county Dublin in the nineteenth century

Lucan as it grew in size in medieval times attracted a number of artisans, who carried on their trade in the village and supplied essential services to its tenants. For example, a survey of County Dublin carried out in 1650-1652 identified Lucan as one of the larger parish settlements.[77] In addition to the presence of gentry, small farmers and labourers, there was also a range of specialised artisans living and working in Lucan, including the maltster (or brewer), the mason, the slater, the butcher and the innkeeper.

A constant element in the development of Lucan has been the river Liffey, which has been crucial to its history. Originally the river ran south to Wexford, but during the Ice Age it changed course, and entered County Dublin at Leixlip, flowing through Lucan and on to the sea. The river has brought social and economic benefits to the area, particularly by providing Lucan with an abundant supply of fast flowing water.

During the seventeenth and eighteenth centuries, a number of industries which were dependent on water were established along the banks of the river Liffey. The mills themselves were built on appropriate sites along the river, and the location of

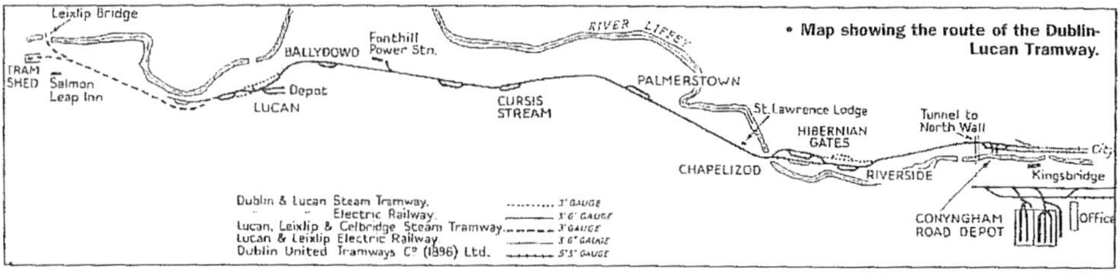

Figure 7: Map showing the route of the Dublin-Lucan Tramway

other mills was always taken into account when choosing the site of a new mill. The presence of the Quaker community was a feature of life in Lucan at this time, as they tended to concentrate their business efforts in Ireland in milling, particularly flour milling.[78] For a considerable time in the eighteenth and nineteenth centuries the river was also important in attracting tourists along the road through the Strawberry Beds to Lucan.

In Lucan Sisson's linen mill was located at Bleach Green, at the bottom of Weir View, from the middle of the eighteenth century. The linen industry in Ireland was built up by weavers who came from France after the revocation of the edict of Nantes in 1594, and this situation was encouraged by the Government. In 1708 spinning schools were established and the Irish Linen Board was established by an Act of Parliament in 1711, enabling the promotion of the linen industry by landowners throughout Ireland.

Bleach Green was generally the name given to the area close to the river where the washing of the linen cloth took place, and the name has remained in Lucan, even though the industry is long gone. The bleaching of linen was a very time consuming process which needed a good supply of running water, and often children as young as nine or ten were involved in the work.

Also, from about 1750 onwards, there was a general improvement in Irish prosperity, including a revival in agriculture because of encouragement of the pre-Grattan Parliament to tillage, through the provision of corn bounties, and to the linen industry which steadily increased in volume.[79] An indication of the scale of the industry in Ireland is that 1.7 million yards of cloth were exported in 1710, while by 1779 this had risen to 18.8 million yards.[80] However, the Linen Board was not successful in its attempts to regulate linen production in Ireland, and it was disbanded in 1828. This development reflected a shift in the balance of power away from landowning and Government interests to the drapers and bleachers of Ulster, who by then were in control of the majority of production.[81]

At the time of the Act of Union in 1801, Lucan was described as having eight wheels for iron work, one grist mill, one corn mill and one paper mill,[82] while

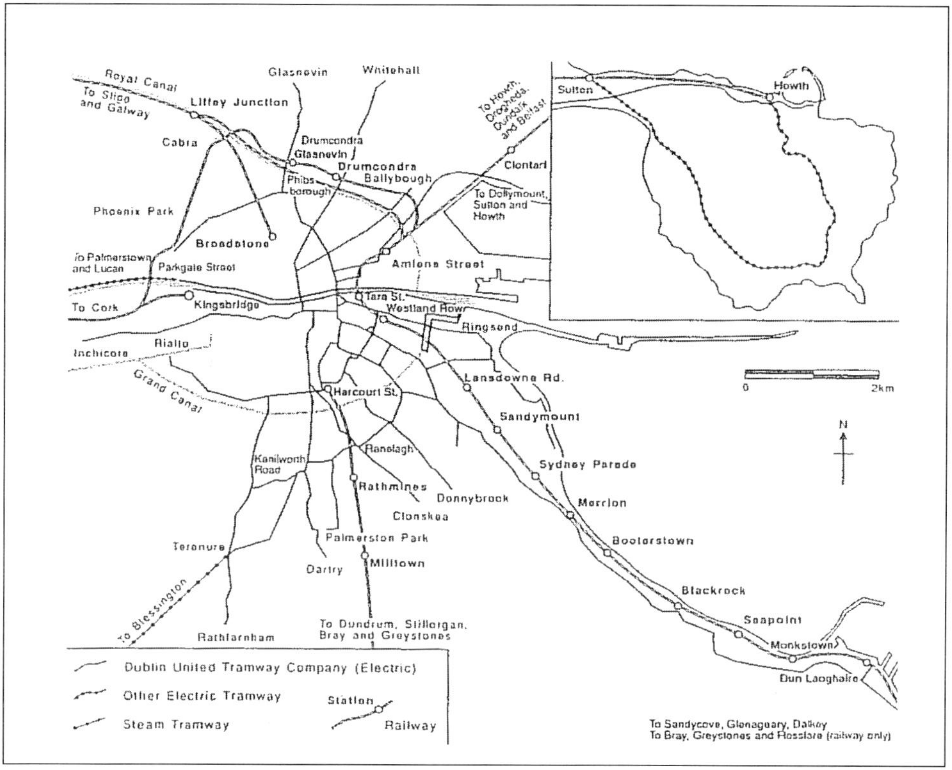

Figure 8: Passenger tramways and railways in 1908

Pigot's Directory of Ireland (1824) noted that there was an extensive linen manufactory and an iron foundry, which afforded employment to the neighbouring poor. Seven years later, the 1831 Census stated that Lucan contained an iron mills employing 20 persons, and a cotton works further up the river whose removal seriously damaged the town and the neighbourhood.

As well as being on one of the major roads of the Slighe road system, Lucan was one of the stops for coach travel on the road west to Sligo and to Galway . This was most important for those travelling west, and also for travel out to Lucan from Dublin city. At one time it was a Royal Mail collection point, and in 1824 the Post Office was open from 7 am to 10 pm.[83] A letter posted in Lucan at 5 pm would arrive at its destination in Galway at 9 pm, quite remarkable by modern day standards.

Two railways served the Lucan area in the mid-nineteenth century. The Great Southern and Western Railway ran just two miles away from the village, and the

Plate 6: The Coffee House, Lucan, County Dublin. Drawing by Suzanne Pegley

Midland and Great Western railway was within one mile of Lucan. These railways replaced sparse services on passenger barges which had been provided on the Royal and Grand canals,[84] and the limited service offered by mail coaches. An indication of the cost is that in 1848, a return trip to the Lucan races cost 1s. 6d. in first class, or 1s.0d. in second class.[85]

By the end of the century, there was a need for improved transport facilities to meet the needs of industries such as Shackletons and Hills. The Dublin and Lucan Steam Tramway Company was founded in 1880 with capital of £30,000,[86] and in 1881 the Dublin and Lucan steam tramway started operations.[87] The initial route to Lucan was later extended to west of the Salmon Leap Inn. By the late 1880s the Lucan, Leixlip and Celbridge Steam Tramway Company proposed extending the line, but this never happened.

The tram ran from Conyngham Road to Lucan until 1900, when electricity replaced steam and the Dublin and Lucan Electric Railway was established, leading to faster speeds and shorter journey times for travellers. The Lucan trams ran until March 1940, when they ceased operation due to increased competition from buses.

At certain times in Ireland, during the nineteenth century, the establishment of mills led to the creation of 'industrial villages' such as Milltown and Rockbrook, around the mills, but in Lucan this did not happen, and the industries remained on the outskirts of the village itself.[88] These two mills, Hill's woollen mills (1859) and Shackleton's flour mills (1860), were both owned by prosperous Quaker merchants, and they provided the majority of local employment. Employers like the Shackletons and the Hills took an interest in their employees' welfare. Social outings were regularly arranged for the employees and their families, and they sometimes provided schooling for the families of workers.

The Shackleton family also owned a number of houses in the village and in Pettycannon, including Canonbrook House and the Hollow. The family built houses for employees on Mount Joseph, the row of houses at the foot of Tinker's Hill, and were responsible, along with the Hill family, for the building of the Coffee House, with a view to keeping the workers away from the public houses, especially on Sundays. The Coffee House was the location of concerts and dances, when visits to the springs were at their height, but this building was demolished in 1984 as part of the redevelopment of the area.

The Anna Liffey mill dates back to the 1820s. This site was chosen because it was one of the few places where a weir could be built on the river to improve the water flow without interfering with the water supply of other mills.[89] The Anna Liffey mill changed hands a number of times before Joseph Shackleton from Ballytore, Co Kildare leased the mill in 1859, for a term of 60 years at £200 per annum. At this time he already had two other corn mills near Lucan, at the 12th and 13th locks of the Grand Canal.

Shackleton's mill produced Lily of the Valley flour, semolina, ground rice and wheatmeal. The mill provided good employment and housing for many local families until it reduced its workforce in 1974 and the business was subsequently sold to Roma Foods in 1978. Although this mill has always been associated with Lucan, it is in fact located in the barony of Castleknock and the parish of Clonsilla.[90]

Today Chadwicks industrial complex, and the economic complex at Lucan Bridge are the only evidence of the area's industrial past. The disused Anna Liffey mill, however, remains as one of only six still in existence in Ireland, and it was bought by Fingal County Council in April 2000. The Council has recently announced plans to restore this mill to good working order, and to develop a living museum of the industrial age in Lucan. This will create an important link with the past, and should provide the inhabitants of Lucan and further afield with an understanding and appreciation of the workings of a large mill.

CONCLUSION

Lucan has a rich and diverse history, and the village can trace its origins back to Early Christian times. There has been a settlement at Lucan since then, and the site was particularly favoured by the Anglo Normans for its strategic location on the banks of the river Liffey. This continuity of settlement continued during the medieval period, and the manor of Lucan created by Henry II was held by the de Peche family for almost one hundred years. The river Liffey has played a key role in the development of Lucan over the years, most notably for its significance in the establishment of a number of industries which rely on the availability of an abundant supply of fast-flowing water.

The castle built at this site, as part of the Anglo Norman aim to secure the area, formed part of a chain of fortresses along the edges of the Pale which were used to control and to defend their lands. Lucan, having originally been on the edge of the Dyflinarskiri, or Viking kingdom of Ireland, was later also situated at the edge of the Pale during Norman times. As such, it was subject to numerous raids from Gaelic tribes in the Dublin mountains, and defence was an important consideration for its inhabitants for many years, particularly in the fourteenth century.

The rise of the Irish nobility was reflected in the granting, in the late fourteenth century, of the manor of Lucan to the Fitzgerald family, who as Earls of Kildare, were to hold a significant position in Irish life until the mid-sixteenth century. Their loss of power, as a result of the Silken Thomas rebellion, allowed other families to fill the vacuum, and the most notable were the Sarsfields, who took possession of the castle at Lucan and whose descendants built Lucan House, still in existence today. The village of Lucan was fortunate, as were other county Dublin villages in the baronies of Newcastle and Uppercross, in avoiding the worst of the ravages of the Cromwellian period in sixteenth century Irish history.

There has been economic activity in Lucan since medieval times, particularly based in the manorial centre which grew up around the medieval manor of Lucan. The development of industry in the seventeenth and eighteenth centuries was made possible through the proximity of the river Liffey. This has provided an important link through the centuries for social and economic development.

More recently, Lucan, along with many other villages in county Dublin, has become a commuter town on the outskirts of Dublin city. The population of the area has increased in size and in diversity, and the majority of its inhabitants travel to the city to work. Substantial development has taken place in the area surrounding the medieval centre of the village, and the history of Lucan through the centuries may not always be apparent to newcomers to the area. It is our hope that this book will provide residents with a greater appreciation of the rich and varied history which underpins the modern village of Lucan in the twenty first century.

Bibliography

Primary Manuscript Sources

Calendar of Ormond Deeds

N.L.I., D422, 'Bond between Margery Tirel and her son William Pecch and his heirs of the rent of 4 marks a year while she lives, c.1295'.

N.L.I., D603, 'Royal licence to John de Hanstede to enfeoff Robert de Nottingham (Notyngham) in the manor of Lucan, 1315'.

N.L.I., D604, 'John de Hanstede grants, releases and quitclaims to Robert de Notyngham and his heirs and assigns all claims to the water mill at Lotereleston, 1315'.

N.L.I., D605, 'Quitclaim from John de Hanstede to Robert de Notyngham, 1315'.

N.L.I., D606, 'Grant of manor of Lucan in the seignory of Meigne, 1315'.

N.L.I., D607, 'Indenture with regard to the manor of Lyuecan between John de Hanstede and Robert de Nottingham, 1315'.

N.L.I., D618, 'David Styward grants to Robert de Notynghame, citizen of Dublin, one burgage in the town of Lyuechan, 1316'.

N.L.I., D847, 'Final concord in the court of the king in the fifteenth year of the reign of Edward III between Simon FitzRichard (plaintiff) and John de Bath and Eglentina on the manor of Lucan and a mill at Lutereleston, 1341'.

De Vesci Papers, N.L.I. Ms. Collection List 89, pp.120-127.

Giraldus Cambrensis, Topographia Hiberniae Ms. 700.

Walshe, R. D., Walshe, Manuscript Collection N.L.I. Ms. 11,657 – 11,658.

Map of lands of Lucan (1680), De Vesci Papers, N.L.I. Ms. 39,256/1.

Primary Printed Sources

Curtis, Edmund, *Calendar of Ormond Deeds, Vol. 1, 1172-1350* (Dublin, 1933).

Lewis, Samuel, *Topographical Dictionary of Ireland, 1837* (London, 1837).

Morrin, James, *Calendar of the Patent and Close Rolls of Chancery in Ireland* (Dublin, 1861).

Pender, Seamus (ed.) *A Census of Ireland c.1659* (Maryland, 1997).

Petty, Dr. William, *The History of the Survey of Ireland AD 1655-56* (commonly called the *Down Survey*) (New York, 1967).

Scott, A.B. and Martin, F.X. (eds), *Expughatio Hibernica The Conquest of Ireland by Giraldus Cambrensis*, vol. 3 (Dublin, 1978).

Simington, Robert, *The Civil Survey AD 1654-1656, vol. vii, County of Dublin* (Dublin, 1945).

Secondary Sources

Aalen, F.H.A., and Whelan, K. (eds), *Dublin City and County: From Prehistory to Present* (Dublin, 1992).

Andrews, J.H., 'A geographer's view of Irish history' in Moody, T.W. and Martin, F.X. (ed.) *The Course of Irish History* (Cork, 1967).

Ball, Francis Elerington, *A History of the County of Dublin* (Dublin, 1906).
Clark, P., (ed.) *The Cambridge Urban History of Britain*, 1540-1840 (Cambridge, 2000).
Cosgrove, Art (ed), *A New History of Ireland, II, Medieval Ireland* 169-1534, (Oxford, 1987).
Curtis, Edmund, *A History of Medieval Ireland* (London, 1923).
Curtis, Edmund, and McDowell, R. B., *Irish Historical Documents*, 1172-1922 (London, 1943).
D'Alton, John, *A History of County Dublin* (Dublin, 1838).
Donegan, Fr Wm. S., *Lucania* (Dublin, 1902).
Ellis, Steven G., *Tudor Ireland: Crown, Community and the Conflict of Culture, 1470-1603* (London, 1985).
Flanagan, Deirdre and Flanagan, Laurence, *Irish Place Names*, (Dublin, 1994).
Gilbert, J. T., *Documents of Ireland* (London, 1870).
Gillham, J., *Dublin United Tramways Co. (1896) Ltd.* (London, 1981).
Graham, B.J. and Proudfoot, L.J., 'Early Medieval Ireland, Settlement c.500-c.1100' in B.J. Graham, (ed.), *An Historical Geography of Ireland* (London, 1993).
Graham, B.J. and Proudfoot, L.J., 'Property, Society and Improvement, c.1700-c.1900' in B.J. Graham, (ed.), *An Historical Geography of Ireland* (London, 1993).
Halliday, Charles, *The Scandinavian Kingdom of Dublin* (Shannon, 1969).
Hogg, W. E., *The Millers and Mills of Ireland of about 1850* (Dublin, 1997).
Joyce, Weston St. John, *Lucan and its Neighbourhood* (Dublin, 1901).
Kilroy, James, *Irish Trams* (Dublin, 1996).
Lawrence, Wm., *List of Photographs of Portraits* (1872).
Lewis, Samuel, *Topographical Dictionary of Ireland* (London, 1837).
Longfield, A.K., *Linen and Cotton Printing in the Eighteenth Century* (place, date).
Maxwell, Constantia, *Irish History from Contemporary Sources, 1509-1610* (London, 1923).
Mulhall, Mary, (ed.), *Lucan and Lucanians, A Revised History of Lucan* (Naas, 1996).
Newham, A.T., *The Dublin and Lucan Tramway. Locomotion Papers* (Dublin, 1964).
O'Keeffe, Peter, *Ireland's Principal Roads 123 AD-1608* (Dublin, 2001).
O'Rourke, John Canon, 'Leixlip Castle and the Valley of the Liffey', *Irish Ecclesiastical Record*, 3rd series, vol. vi, no. 1 (1885).
Otway-Ruthven, A. J., *A History of Medieval Ireland* (London, 1968).
Pigot's *Directory of Ireland*, 1824.
Smith, William J., *Map-making Landscapes and Memory; a Geography of Colonial and Early Modern Ireland c. 1530-1750* (Cork, 2006).
Todhunter, John, *Life of P. Sarsfield, earl of Lucan: with a short narrative of the principal events of the Jacobite war in Ireland* (Dublin, 1895).
Wauchope, Piers, *Patrick Sarsfield and the Williamite Wars* (Dublin, 1922).
Young, Arthur, *A Tour in Ireland* (2nd ed., Belfast, 1983).

Papers

Doherty, C., 'Early Irish towns' presented to Colloquy on Irish towns in medieval Europe 900-1250 AD (Dublin, 1978).

Articles in Irish Periodicals

Doherty, C., 'Exchange and Trade in early Medieval Ireland' in *Journal of Royal Society of Antiquaries*, vol. 110 (1980), pp. 67-89.

'Fisheries on the river Liffey. Notes on Corporation Fisheries from the dissolution of the monasteries' in *Journal of Royal Society of Antiquaries in Ireland.* Vol. lxxxiv, part l (1954), pp.41—58.

Graham, B. J., *Medieval Irish Settlements: A Review in Historical Geography Research*, Series no. 3.

Hayes, Richard J., *Sources for the History of Irish Civilisation. Places and Dates.*

'Irish Health Resorts' in the *Catholic Bulletin*, vol.V., (August, 1915) pp.624-627.

'Lucan, Swift's Hospital for Lunatics. Purchase of building/land near Lucan' in the *Irish Builder*, vol. xi, no. 922, p.78.

'Manor of Lucan and Restoration Land Settlement' in the *Dublin Historical Record*, vol. xxi, no. 4, (September 1967) pp.139-143.

Mills, J., 'Tenants and Agriculture near Dublin in the Fourteenth Century' in the *Journal of the Royal Society of Antiquaries in Ireland*, vol xxi (1890-1891), pp 54-63.

Mills, J., 'The Norman Settlement in Leinster – the Cantreds near Dublin' in the *Journal of the Royal Society of Antiquaries*, vol. iv (1894), pp.161-175.

Newham, A.T., The Dublin and Lucan Tramway in the *Locomotion Papers*, (Dublin, 1964).

Unpublished works

Collins, Dolores, 'The Anna Liffey Mill, Lucan: Shackleton Period: 1859-1978' (M.A. thesis NUI Maynooth, 2004).

Pegley, Suzanne, 'Road networks: From turnpike to motorway, Case study of Leixlip and Lucan' (NUI Maynooth, 2004).

Pegley, Suzanne, 'The Development of Lucan'. (NUI Maynooth, 2004).

Footnotes

1. Anngret Simms and Patricia Fagan, 'Villages in County Dublin: their origins and inheritance' in Aalen, F.H.A., and Whelan, K., (eds.), *Dublin City and County: From Prehistory to Present* (Dublin, 1992), p.91.
2. William J. Smyth, 'Exploring the social and cultural topographics of sixteenth and seventeenth century county Dublin' in Aalen & Whelan, *Dublin City and County,* p.121.
3. Deirdre Flanagan and Laurence Flanagan, *Irish Place Names* (Dublin, 1994).
4. P. O'Keeffe, *Ireland's Principal Roads 123 AD – 1608* (Dublin, 2001), pp.67-85.
5. Edmund Curtis, *A History of Medieval Ireland* (London, 1938), p.xxxiv.
6. *Irish Names of Places*, vol 1, p. 402, in Weston St John Joyce, *Lucan and its Neighbourhoods* (Dublin, 1901).
7. E. Curtis, *A History of Medieval Ireland* (London, 1923), p.xxxv.
8. Walshe Manuscript Collection, Leixlip and Lucan (N.L.I., MS 11658).
9. B.J. Graham, *Medieval Irish Settlements, A Review in Historical Geography Research,* Series no. 3, p.9.
10. Simms & Fagan, 'Villages in county Dublin' in Aalen & Whelan, *Dublin City and County,* p.91.
11. Liam De Paor, *Peoples of Ireland: from prehistory to modern times* (London, 1986), p.99.
12. Tadhg O'Keeffe, 'Medieval frontiers and fortifications: The Pale and its evolution' in Aalen & Whelan *Dublin City and County,* p.58.
13. B.J. Graham, *Medieval Irish Settlements,* p.7.
14. ibid., p.9.
15. Edmund Curtis, *Calendar of Ormond Deeds, vol. 1, 1172-1350* (Dublin, 1933), p.v.
16. ibid., p.3.
17. John Watt, *The Church in Medieval Ireland* (Dublin, 1972).
18. Walshe Manuscript Collection (NLI MS 11,658).
19. John Bradley, 'The topographical development of Scandinavian Dublin' in Aalen & Whelan, *Dublin City and County,* p.49.
20. Simms & Fagan, 'Villages in county Dublin' in Aalen & Whelan, *Dublin City and County,* p.91.
21. ibid., p.93.
22. *Burgage*: tenure under which property of the king or the lord in a town or village was held in return for a yearly rent, or the rendering of a service.
23. J. T. Gilbert, *Documents of Ireland* (London, 1870), p.372.
24. James Mills, 'Tenants and Agriculture near Dublin in the Fourteenth Century' in *Journal of the Royal Society of Antiquaries*, vol xxi (1890-1891), p.54.
25. J.A. Watt, 'The Anglo-Irish colony under strain 1327-1399', in Cosgrove A. (ed), *A New History of Ireland, II, Medieval Ireland 1169-1534* (Oxford, 1987), p.353.
26. Tadhg O'Keeffe, 'Medieval frontiers and fortifications: The Pale and its evolution' in Aalen & Whelan, *Dublin City and County,* p.66.
27. A. Cosgrove, 'The Emergence of the Pale, 1399-1447' in idem (ed), *A New History*

of Ireland, p.533.

28. ibid., p.537.
29. ibid., p.563.
30. B.J. Graham, *Medieval Irish Settlements*, p.7.
31. William J. Smyth, 'sixteenth and seventeenth century county Dublin' in Aalen & Whelan, *Dublin City and County*, p.174.
32. Simms & Fagan, 'Villages in county Dublin' in Aalen & Whelan, *Dublin City and County*, p.100.
33. ibid., p.101.
34. Appendix A & B, Upper Cross and Newcastle and Upper Cross Baronies, Book of Reference of Down Survey Maps in Robert Simington, *The Civil Survey AD 1654-1656, vol. vii, County of Dublin* (Dublin, 1945), pp 287-317.
35. *Feoffee*: person who had been granted land through feoffment, the gift or conveyance in fee of land or other goods.
36. Curtis, *Calendar of Ormond Deeds*, p.4.
37. ibid., p.4.
38. H. S. Sweetman (ed.), *Calendar of Documents relating to Ireland* no. 192, 197 in James Mills, 'The Norman Settlement in Leinster- The Cantreds near Dublin', *Journal of the Royal Society of Antiquaries*, vol. xxi (1894), p. 170.
39. *Palfrey*: everyday riding horse, often used by a woman.
40. *Curtilage*: enclosed area occupied by a dwelling, grounds and outbuildings.
41. B.J. Graham, *Medieval Irish Settlements*, p.21.
42. Simms & Fagan, 'Villages in county Dublin' in Aalen & Whelan *Dublin City and County*, p.109.
43. *Kildare Archaeological Society Journal*, vol. xvi, p.417.
44. *Feudal tenure*: in the Middle Ages, a tenant held land in return for agricultural or other non-military service, or for payment of rent monies.
45. *Escheator*: person handling the reversion of the property to the Crown, particularly in cases where the deceased had no legal heirs, or whose heirs were not of age.
46. James Mills, 'The Norman Settlement in Leinster- The Cantreds near Dublin', *JRSA*, vol. xxiv (1894), p.174.
47. ibid., p.175.
48. 'Royal licence to John de Hanstede to enfeoff Robert de Nottingham (Notyngham) in the manor of Lucan, 1315' (N.L.I., MS D603).
49. *In capite*: a tenancy by which land was held either by knight's service or socage (the performance of specified services or payment of rent, with no obligation to military service).
50. *Quit claim*: formal statement renouncing a legal claim previously made.
51. *Messuages*: a dwelling and its lands, including outbuildings.
52. 'John de Hanstede grants, releases and quitclaims to Robert de Notyngham and his heirs and assigns all claims to the water mill at Lotereleston, 1315' (N.L.I., MS D604).

53. 'Indenture with regard to the manor of Lyuecan between John de Hanstede and Robert de Nottingham, 1315' (N.L.I., MS D607).
54. 'David Styward grants to Robert de Notynghame, citizen of Dublin, one burgage in the town of Lyuechan, 1316' (N.L.I., MS D618).
55. *Seisin*: legal freehold possession of the land.
56. John D'Alton, *A History of County Dublin* (Dublin, 1838), p.658.
57. John Canon O'Rourke, 'Leixlip Castle and the Valley of the Liffey', *Irish Ecclesiastical Record,* 3rd series, vol. vi, no. 1 (1885), p. 27.
58. Calendar of Patent Rolls I (1861), p.317.
59. Fr W. S. Donegan, *Lucania* (Dublin, 1902).
60. S. Pegley, 'The Development of Lucan' (unpublished paper, NUI Maynooth, 2004).
61. Samuel Lewis, *Topographical Dictionary of Ireland* (London, 1837), p.320.
62. ibid., p.321.
63. John D'Alton, *History of County Dublin* (Dublin, 1838), p.655.
64. Donegan, *Lucania*, p.1.
65. P. Clark, (ed.), *The Cambridge Urban History of Britain, 1540-1840* (Cambridge, 2000) p.776.
66. Walshe Collection (N.L.I. MS 11,657-8).
67. John D'Alton, *History of County Dublin (Dublin*, 1938), p.662.
68. Walshe Collection (N.L.I. MS 11,657-8).
69. Pegley, 'The Development of Lucan'.
70. *Sunday Freeman*, 19th October 1913.
71. Named for Major General J.A. Hanbury of the Army and Navy Club, London, a close friend of the Vesey family, owners of Lucan House.
72. Chapel Hill, the new main road, was constructed in 1837.
73. The small lane to the weir, opposite St Andrew's Church, created when a bridge was built over the river at this location.
74. Originally named for the tinkers who camped there at one time.
75. Simms & Fagan, 'Villages in county Dublin' in Aalen & Whelan, *Dublin City and County,* p.93.
76. William J. Smyth, 'sixteenth and seventeenth century county Dublin' in Aalen & Whelan, *Dublin City and County,* p.126.
77. ibid., p.155.
78. Aalen & Whelan, *Dublin City and County,* p.2.
79. Arthur Young, *A Tour in Ireland* (2nd ed., Belfast, 1983), p.viii.
80. ibid., p.221.
81. B.J. Graham, and L.J. Proudfoot, 'Property, Society and Improvement, c.1700 - c.1900' in B.J. Graham, (ed.), *An Historical Geography of Ireland* (London, 1993), p.234.
82. Mary Mulhall, *Lucan and Lucanians: A Revised History of Lucan* (Dublin, 1996), p.19.
83. *Pigot's Directory of Ireland* (1827), p.167.
84. James Killen, 'Transport in Dublin: Past, Present and Future' in Aalen & Whelan

Dublin City and County, p.306.

85. Walshe Manuscript Collection (N.L.I. MS 11,658). .
86. A.T. Newham, *The Dublin and Lucan Tramway Locomotion Papers* (Dublin, 1964).
87. James Kilroy, *Irish Trams* (Dublin, 1996), p.46.
88. ibid., p.104.
89. Dolores Collins, 'The Anna Liffey Mill, Lucan: Shackleton Period, 1859-1978' (M.A. thesis, NUI Maynooth, 2004), p.16.
90. ibid., p.11.

ST. ANDREW'S LUCAN – HISTORY, ARCHITECTURE *and* ARTWORKS

by Valerie Twomey

INTRODUCTION - THE CHRISTIAN PARISH AND LOCAL HISTORY

The importance of the Christian parish, as a focus of analysis and as a source of historical records in the practice of local history in Ireland, cannot be underestimated. The Christian parish, i.e. a pastoral ministry for a defined local area as opposed to the previous monastic based approach to local ministry, has been a feature of the social and physical landscape of Ireland for approximately one thousand years. The Christian parish provides three important historical sources of evidence to the local historian. Firstly, the administrative records of christenings, weddings and funerals help to trace the major life events of individual parishioners over many generations.[1] Secondly, the succession lists and biographies of the priests and incumbents cast light on the evolution of the church as an institution.[2] Finally the study of the location, design, financing, architecture, décor and artworks of parish churches i.e. the building legacy of the Christian parish, and their associated files and other records, provides important insights into legal history, architectural history, the study of material culture and the history of art amongst other topics.[3] Such site specific studies also have a significant economic history dimension in that the construction or renovation of a church, in any age, is an expensive endeavour and as the marriage service in the Church of Ireland notes 'it is one not to be undertaken lightly'.

While the building legacy may be the most visible manifestation on the landscape of the Christian parish, the history of parishes is however primarily about people – the people who initially built and endowed the parish church, the people who minister and worship in it and the people who strive, often for their entire life and in the case of some families over several generations, to sustain their parish church over time. Most of these people are volunteers, in many cases nameless to later generations, who dedicated their time and talents to this noble purpose. The story of the construction and subsequent evolution of St Andrew's Church of Ireland in Lucan, built in 1823 is one such multi-layered story. It is a story of people, art and architecture, worship and ongoing dedicated local involvement in the maintenance of not just an important historic building, but it is also a story of a changing and evolving community over a period of nearly two hundred years.

THE CHURCHES OF LUCAN

Churches are amongst the major visual features in both the rural and urban Irish landscape. In every part of Ireland they can be seen, either as picturesque ruins or as functioning landmark buildings. Lucan is no exception to this pattern. Today there are eight church sites located in the Lucan/Esker area. The churches of Lucan range from the early medieval ruins of St Finian's church in Esker to the new Roman Catholic Church of St Patrick in Esker which was opened in 1985. These buildings were built at various times over the last millennium to serve the religious needs of the people of Lucan, Esker and Dodsborough. Today the church architectural heritage in Lucan includes four gems of nineteenth century church architecture. Three of these buildings are located in the heart of old Lucan village and one is located on the hill overlooking the village. They are St Andrew's Church of Ireland 1823, St Mary's Roman Catholic Church 1835-40, Lucan Methodist Church 1877 and Lucan Presbyterian Church (totally remodelled except for the façade in 1988). Each building is unique and each represents aspects of the social

Plate 1: View of St Andrew's Church Lucan 2007

and ecclesiastical history of its own denomination in the last two centuries.[4] The process of building, erecting and maintaining a church building is never ending as evidenced by the fact that all four of these nineteenth century churches have undergone major development projects in the last twenty years. In this spirit of moving with the times it is hoped that there will be a new church presence (most likely on a shared interdenominational basis) in the new communal buildings now under construction in Adamstown, thereby continuing a millennium long tradition of church building in Lucan.

This essay describes St Andrew's Church of Ireland - one of these wonderful nineteenth century examples of Church architecture. The essay commences with a brief history of the Church of Ireland parish in Lucan and Leixlip[5] and describes St Andrew's, firstly in the context of the Church of Ireland architectural style of the early nineteenth century and the influence that this had on the initial design, construction and its financing. The issue of the possible involvement of James Gandon in the design of St Andrew's is also considered. Later sections review the evolution of the fabric of the building through at least five distinct phases over the last 184 years. The essay concludes with a description of some of the more important decorative and artwork features of St Andrew's, including two important twentieth century stained glass windows and a number of family monuments associated with the Vesey and Needham families.

Plate 2: St Finian's church Esker

The ancient pre-Norman Esker Riada, the main road from Dublin to the Shannon and onwards to the west of Ireland, probably went through the Esker/South Lucan area near St Finian's church.[6] Prior to the reformation there were two parish churches in the Lucan/Esker area - St Finian's in Esker and the Church of the Blessed Virgin Mary near Lucan Castle in the village of Lucan. Both of these churches are now in ruins and they have not been used as churches for more than two centuries although the attached graveyards continued in use well into the twentieth century.

Plate 3: Church of the Blessed Virgin Mary, Lucan

One of the earliest references to the parish of Lucan records the granting of the advowson (the right to nominate the clergy to a vacant office) of the church of the Blessed Virgin Mary in the early part of the thirteenth century by Wirris Peche to the priory of St Catherine when it was recorded as having a value of eighteen marks. After the dissolution of St Thomas's Abbey (which then controlled the advowsons of St Catherine's) the revenue of the church became impropriate (i.e. it passed out of the hands of the church to a lay owner) and was leased by the crown to Sir William Sarsfield. (ref. Suzanne Pegley's essay which details the role of the Sarsfield family in the history of Lucan). Early in the seventeenth century both the nave and the chancel of the Church of the Blessed Virgin Mary were reported as being in good repair, however by 1630 the chancel had become 'ruinous'. The then vicar Thomas Keating was recorded as being married to a recusant (i.e. a Roman Catholic) and the value of the parish was reckoned at only £10 as there were not more that five Protestant parishioners. Both of these ancient churches probably went out of active use in the mid-seventeenth century. After the Restoration in the 1660s, the parish of Lucan was united with Leixlip and remained so until the dis-establishment of the Church of Ireland in 1871 when it became a separate parish. In the period 1823-1871 the parish of Leixlip had the one rector but it was organised into two sub units – viz. Leixlip and Lucan. In 1918 the two parishes were re-united as a single union and have remained so until today. In the current organisation structure of the Church of Ireland the united parishes, now known as Leixlip Union, constitute the most north-western parish in the diocese of Glendalough within the united archdiocese of Dublin and Glendalough.[7]

CHURCH OF IRELAND BUILDING IN THE EARLY NINETEENTH CENTURY

Following the passing of Act of Union in 1800 the Church of Ireland received substantial funds from the government in London for a major nation-wide church building programme. These monies were routed through the Board of First Fruits Commissioners. In 1829 it was estimated that the board had received funds of circa £700,000 in the period 1808-29. This largesse enabled the board to support the construction of 633 parish churches as well as more than 500 glebe houses in that period.[8] These churches were mostly the simple tower-and-hall structures familiar in the Irish countryside today - the so-called 'First Fruits Gothic' style. These were small sturdy unassuming buildings with a square west tower, a rectangular hall/nave often with a small west gallery, pointed windows and a shallow rectangular sanctuary. First fruit churches were usually built of local rubble stone and were invariably rendered in lime plaster. The principal architect of the board was John Bowden and by 1830 an architect had been appointed for each province of the Church of Ireland. However, it is difficult in most instances in the absence of other corroborative evidence, to ascribe particular examples of first fruit churches to individual architects. The board made both loans and grants to individual parishes to support the construction of these churches. The repayment rate was initially set at six percent and this was later reduced to four percent and the typical grant was for £500. Wealthy parishes were expected to fund their own building programmes but more often the cost of construction was made up of a grant and long-term loans from the board with the balance being financed by parishioner donations and or by local benefactors. As we shall see this was the case in Lucan.

The extra financial support provided by benefactors or access to architectural expertise, allowed parishes to build more elaborate churches than the standard first fruits gothic style. In particular the addition of a spire was always a desirable, but expensive option. Where resources allowed, elaborate interiors or additional exterior features were also inserted. As we shall see in the case of St Andrew's these additions extended to the construction of a tall spire and two elegant galleries.[9] It was the policy of the board to position new churches in prominent sites to emphasise the power and prestige of the established church. Consequently many of the country first fruits churches are beautifully sited and a favoured option was to locate the church either within, or contiguous to, ancient or medieval graveyards or ruins. The intention being to emphasise the continuity and line of succession of the Church of Ireland in the rural or village landscape and community. In towns, similar objectives applied with prominent sites, important junctions or proximity to the entrance gates to landed estates or demesnes being preferred.

ST ANDREW'S CHURCH LUCAN

At the beginning of the nineteenth century there was no Church of Ireland church in Lucan village. The lack of a church building in Lucan meant that the members of the Church of Ireland who resided in Lucan needed to travel to St Mary's parish church in Leixlip to take part in Sunday worship.[10] The growth in the numbers of Church of Ireland members in the Lucan area and the availability of finance from the Board of First Fruits Commissioners meant that, in the early years of the nineteenth century, the vision of building a Church of Ireland church in Lucan could be realised. In the circumstance it was decided not to restore the Church of the Blessed Virgin Mary located in the grounds of Lucan Demesne and instead the decision was taken to construct a new building.

St Andrew's is located on the main street in what is now known as old Lucan village. In 1831, less than ten years after the church was built, Samuel Lewis recorded that the village of Lucan consisted of 187 houses many of which were fitted out as lodging-houses for the use of the many visitors to the village to 'drink the waters'. Lewis described St Andrew's as 'a neat church with a tower and spire'.[11] In 1831 the

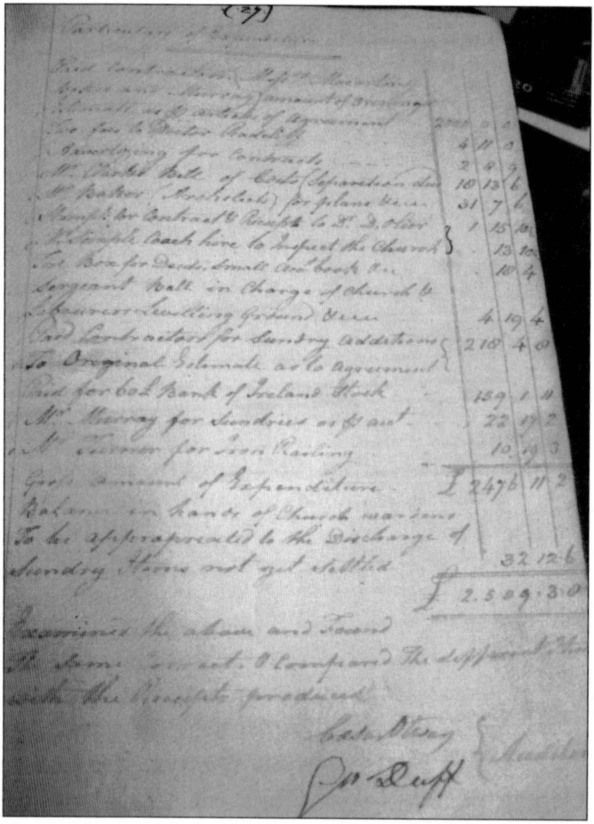

(27)

Particulars of Expenditure

[illegible] Estimate as p articles of agreement	2000	0	0
[illegible] to Doctor [illegible]			
Advertizing for Contracts	4	11	0
Mr. [illegible] Bill of Costs (Separation deed)	2	9	9
	10	13	6
Mr Baker (Architect) for plans &c	31	7	6
Stamps for Contract & Receipts to Dr D. [illegible]	1	15	10
[illegible] Coach hire to Inspect the Church		13	10
[illegible] Box for Deeds, Small [illegible] book &c		10	4
Sergeant Hall in Charge of Church & [illegible] ground &c	4	19	4
Paid Contractors for Sundry additions to Original Estimate as to agreement	218	4	0
Paid for 60£ Bank of Ireland Stock	159	1	11
Mr Murray for Sundries as p acct	22	17	2
Mr [illegible] for Iron Railing	10	19	3
Gross amount of Expenditure	£2476	11	2
Balance in hands of Church wardens To be appropriated to the Discharge of Sundry Items not yet settled	32	12	6
	£2509	3	0

Examined the above and Found the Same Correct & Compared the different Items with the Receipts produced.

Caesar Otway
[illegible] Duff
Auditors

Plate 4: Cost of St Andrew's Church; VMB, 1822 – 2008

number of adherents of the Church of Ireland in the Lucan and Esker area was 531 compared to 314 in Leixlip. In May 1870 the vestry minute books lists fifty vestrymen for the parish of Lucan and the numbers listed varied between forty and forty five over the following twenty years.[12] In this period only men registered formally on the vestry lists. The land on which the new church was eventually built was granted by James Gandon. In line with contemporary practice, the land was granted to a set of trustees who in turn requested the archbishop of Dublin to grant the land to George Vesey and Richard Needham, the then churchwardens and to the incumbent.[13]

On the construction of the new church in Lucan a separate vestry and a perpetual curacy (a permanent benefice where the tithes were held by someone else), within the overall parish of Leixlip Union, was established for Lucan. In effect there were two parishes with the same incumbent, but with a separate curate for Lucan.[14] The first curate for Lucan was the celebrated antiquarian Caesar Otway.[15] In the Church of Ireland most aspects of parish governance are carried out through a group known as the vestry or since 1871 as the select vestry. The vestry minute books for Leixlip Union are extant for this period. These records were retained by the parish of Leixlip Union until 2005 when the parishioners funded some restoration and rebinding work before presenting the bulk of this important source material for the local historian to the Church of Ireland Archive in the Representative Church Body Library (RCBL) where it can be more readily accessed by researchers.[16]

The parish vestry consisted of the clergy, churchwardens and the leading laymen i.e. property owners of the parish. The vestry met several times a year and was primarily charged with overseeing the administration of parish finances with particular reference to the maintenance of parish buildings. From the vestry minute book and other records such as deeds and correspondence files, it is possible to reconstruct many aspects of the process by which St Andrew's was built and financed in the 1820's and the subsequent changes that were made to the building over time, as requirements changed and as resources allowed. It is also possible to trace the activities of and the efforts made by particular individuals to the maintenance and development of their parish church. As with many such sources careful reading is required to extract the maximum information from records that are usually incomplete, are often opaque in their descriptions and lack the detail that would allow for a more forensic examination of the detail. For example the only reference in this period in the Leixlip vestry minutes to the establishment of the new church in Lucan was in June 1822 when it was resolved that 'it appears to this vestry that in consequence of the separation of the union of Leixlip into two separate parish unions that there should be some statement made of the mode in which the above mentioned balance (£118.12s.4d.) and the future collection in this church should be disposed of, it is resolved that the poor of Lucan Union shall receive in as ample a manner as heretofore all the benefits arising from the funds now in hand or in the future to be collected'.

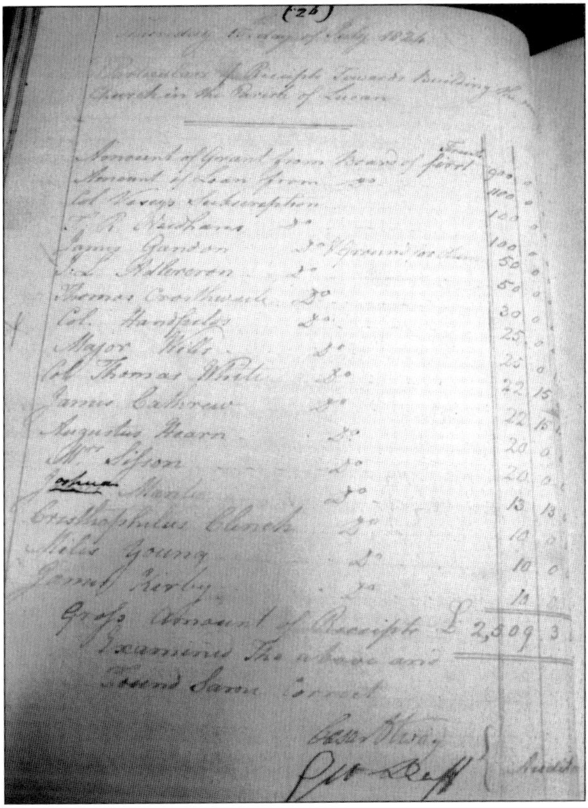
Gross Amount of Receipts £ 2,509 3
Examined the above and Found same Correct

Plate 5: Sources of finance for the construction of St Andrew's Church; VMB, 1822 – 2008

The cost of construction of St Andrew's was £2,509.3s.0d. The Board of First Fruits made a grant of £900 and loan of £1,100.[17] As with other board loans the initial rate was 6% (£60 per annum) which was later reduced to 4% (£40.13s.4d.

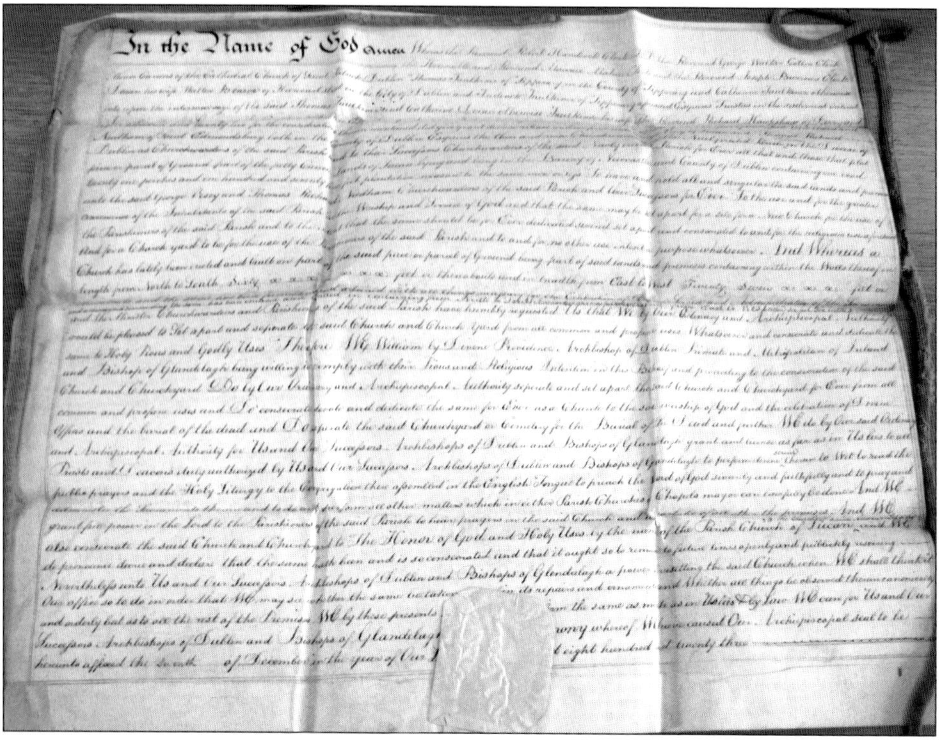

Plate 6: Memorial of dedication of St Andrew's Lucan – RCBL P.0913

per annum). Subscriptions from fifteen named parishioners raised a further £509. Major subscribers included Colonel George Vesey of Lucan House and Thomas Needham of St Edmondsbury who subscribed £100 each and James Gandon of Canonbrook who subscribed £50.[18]

St Andrew's was built by McCartney, Barker & Murray of James's Street Dublin and the architect was Henry Aaron Baker. Building proceeded quickly and on the 11 December 1823 the 'Protestant Parishioners of the Parish of Lucan assembled in Vestry' sent a memorial to William Magee Archbishop of Dublin stating that 'they have agreed to the following appropriation of the Pews of the Church lately erected in said Parish. Subject to your Grace's approbation and Sanction.'[19] The memorial lists thirty-two pews in the body of the church and a further six in the gallery. Each box pew is listed as 'a three seat' giving space for ninety-six attendees in the body of the church and, with an estimated six seats per box in the gallery making a further thirty six, seats giving an overall total capacity of one hundred and thirty two. Exactly half of the seats in the body of the church were allocated to named parishioners including Thomas Richard Needham Esq. (2) and Colonel Vesey (3). The

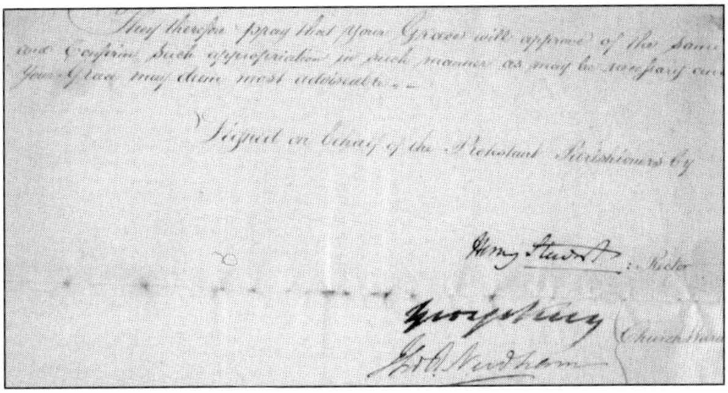
May therefore pray that Your Grace will approve of the same and confirm such appropriation in such manner as may be necessary or Your Grace may deem most advisable. –

Signed on behalf of the Protestant Parishioners by

: Rector

Church Wardens

Plate 7: Signatures on memorial requesting archbishop of Dublin to commission St Andrew's Church Lucan 1823 – RCBL P.0913

churchwardens, the rector and the curate were also allocated a seat each. The six seats in the gallery were allocated to Colonel Vesey, James Gandon Esq., Thomas Richard Needham Esq., Major John Wills. Colonel Handfield and John Aldercorn Esq. The map attached to the memorial clearly shows the galleries placed at either end of the church, the communion table on the east centre of the church and the reading desk opposite it on the west side.

James Gandon (1742-1823) the architect of the Four Courts, the Custom House and the King's Inns shaped Dublin as no other architect.[20] Gandon retired to Lucan in 1805 and died there in December 1823 only a few weeks after the opening of St Andrew's. He built a fine house in Lucan called Canonbrook, which is still in private ownership. James Gandon donated the site on which St Andrew's parish church was built in 1823, made a financial contribution to the project and was a member of the vestry in the years before the construction of St Andrew's. It is believed locally that Gandon was responsible for the design of St Andrew's and Hugo Duffy lists Lucan Church as Gandon's last work although he labels it as 'uncorroborated'. Edward McParland is of the view that the church is sufficiently close to a 1793 drawing in the National Library to conclude that it is at least based on a design by Gandon.[21] Desmond Guinness has also recently asserted Gandon's role.[22] Gandon is known to have designed two other churches viz. the tower at Maryborough (Portlaoise) in

To His Grace William Lord Archbishop of Dublin

Humbly Sheweth –

Gallery

No. 1 Colonel Vesey
2 James Gandon Esqr
3 Thomas Richard Needham Esqr
4 Major John Wills
5 Colonel Handfield
6 John Aldercorn Esqr

Plate 8: List of occupiers of pews St Andrew's Church Lucan 1823 – RCBL P.0913

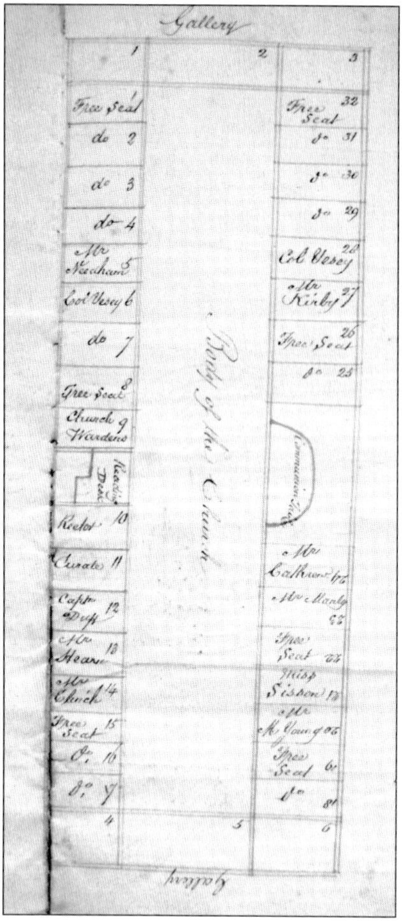

Plate 9: Map of Pews St Andrew's Church, Lucan 1823

1800 and the church at Coolbanagher in County Laois 1781-85. The Church at Coolbanagher has an overall appearance not dissimilar to Lucan; however the tower is more elegant and the internal decorative features are considerably more elaborate with stuccowork and recesses for urns. Henry Aaron Baker was master of the Dublin Society Drawing School for fifty years, he had worked with Gandon for many years and completed Gandon's commission for the King's Inns. He was probably therefore familiar with many of Gandon's church drawings. However, current opinion is that while Baker may have been influenced by Gandon's ideas and may even have discussed the project with his former partner and mentor, that credit for the final design of St Andrew's should go to Baker.

The RCBL archive contains the Act of Consecration of the church in Lucan. This act formally named the new church as St Andrew's, specified the size of the church grounds at two hundred and nine feet and east west eighty six feet six inches and noted that the church dimensions were north south sixty feet and east west twenty seven feet and that it 'has been furnished and adorned with all things necessary for the Celebration of Divine Service and Administration of the Sacraments and a churchyard surrounding the same has been enclosed and walled in' The new church was to be devoted 'for ever' to religious and pious uses and not for 'common and profane uses' and service was to 'perform divine service therein to wit to read the public prayers and the Holy Liturgy to the Congregation there assembled in the English Tounge to preach the Word of God sincerely and faithfully and to pray and administer the Sacraments therein and to do and to perform all other matters which in either Parish Churches or Chapels may or can lawfully be done.'[23]

The issue of the occupation of pews was never far from the minds of the select vestry. In November 1887 the minute book noted that 'A discussion ensued on the subject of the free & open system as against the pew system, on the proposal of the chairman of the following resolution which however was not put to a vote – That it is inexpedient to allocate to any particular person the sittings in the parish church of Lucan which in the course of time may be vacated by their present occupiers – and the word free ought to be attached to such pews as are not allocated. There seemed to be a general wish for further information, & in compliance with the request of some vestrymen the Chairman said he would be glad to preach upon the subject.' At the next meeting in January 1888 the Chairman proposed the same resolution which failed to be passed. There are no later references to this issue in the minutes and one can only assume that the practice of 'free' pews was progressively extended to the entire church as previously allocated pews became available. Indeed the practice of purchased pews had all but disappeared in most parish churches by this time.

ST ANDREW'S 1823-2007 – THE EVOLUTION OF THE BUILDING

While St Andrew's was built in the 1820s, at the height of the Board of First Fruits building boom, and its construction was supported by the board, on closer examination St Andrew's displays features in both its overall design and in the internal fittings which are more complex than the standard hall and tower design of the board's churches. St Andrew's is therefore worthy of more detailed study to establish the original design concept and also to establish a chronology of the changes since 1823. These changes, like those in any building, were driven by the interaction of the changing needs and resources of the parish, contemporary conventions, philosophies and fashion and also the need to maintain fabric degraded by the ravages of time.

St Andrew's displays a mixture of classical features in combination with some signs of the gothic revival that took place in the mid-nineteenth century and which took off in earnest from around 1830. The classical feature included the overall proportions of the box-like hall/nave, the raised and fielded panelling, the facing galleries (north and south) and facing apses (east and west) and the cornices and the vaulted ceiling. It also incorporated a number of gothic features including pointed windows and external pinnacles both on the tower and at the corners of the hall that were common on later churches. Overall however, the conservative neo-classical style of the initial design for St Andrew's with its cross axial and preacher oriented i.e. pulpit internal layout shows little sign of the fashion for gothic that was then beginning to dominate Church architecture. As Craig commented in 1982 'the pulpit was commonly central in the geometrical as well as the moral sense'.[24] St Andrew's is therefore in marked contrast for example to the Chapel Royal in Dublin Castle, built in 1807 by Francis Johnston, which is an outstanding example of gothic

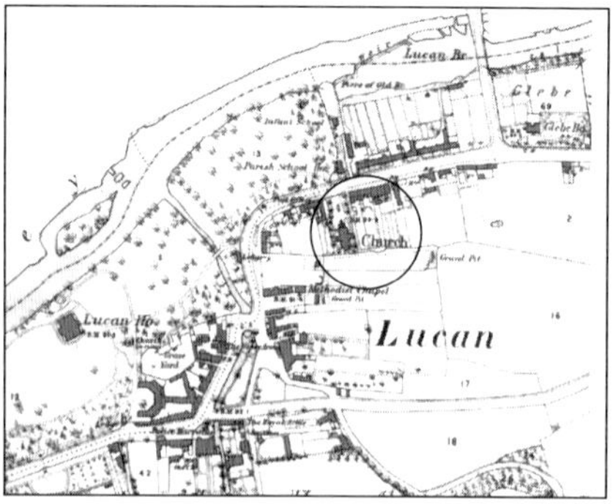

Plate 10: Map of Lucan 1871 – Showing St Andrew's church (circled) and grounds

plasterwork, woodwork, sculpture and glass. Likewise St Andrew's seems to owe nothing to the contemporary more adventurous designs of John Semple, architect for the diocese of Dublin, who built seventeen churches in Dublin and Leinster from the 1820s onwards, most notably the Black Church in Dublin in 1826.[25]

St Andrew's consists of a tower and nave/hall structure with an apse on the east and the west walls. The tower of St Andrew's is aligned with the front gate and is set one hundred feet back from the gate at the highest point of the rising ground. It consists of a two-storey hallway with plain glass gothic windows facing north and east, a belfry storey with large belfry louvers, a clock on the north face and circular openings on each face. The tower is topped with a gothic freeze, parapet and battlements. At each corner of the tower there is a pyramid spire. The tower is topped-off by a spire topped by a ball and weather vane on which is embossed 1823, the year of the church's construction. There is a stringcourse below the battlements at the same level as the roofline of the hall. The windows, louvers and door are surmounted with hooded mouldings. The tower has ashlar quoin stones in limestone. There is a small basement with vaulted ceilings situated under the tower. The basement has been used over the years as the location for heating equipment and as a storage area. The entrance to the basement was sealed off some years ago. The spire dominates the skyline of Lucan village as is evident from photographs from the mid-nineteenth century. The external walls of the hall/nave and tower are rendered in pebbledash throughout. As on the tower, the windows are surmounted by hooded mouldings and the windows have limestone reveals. A stepped parapet, which reflects the battlements on the tower, tops the walls, and there are pyramid spires at each corner. The entrance door is set in the west wall of the porch and the church is entered through a pair of coffered panel doors leading off this porch. The stairs to the first floor balcony has elegant balusters and a mahogany handrail. A steep rough cut stairs ascends to the belfry room. This room has no ceiling and it is possible to see the inside stonework of the spire. The church gates and railings were manufactured by the local Turner ironworks at a cost of forty five guineas.

Five major building phases can be discerned in the evolution of St Andrew's from its initial construction in 1823 to the last major change which took place in 1997. Some of the early phases were surprisingly short with major alterations occurring at only twenty-year intervals in the mid-nineteenth century. The first and second phases - the most classical ones - lasted from 1823 to the late-1860s. The third and fourth phases, involved a radical change to the internal layout in line with the prevailing Pugin influenced gothic oriented design concepts. The internal layout was re-oriented from cross-axial to the nave facing south on the longer axis of the hall. These phases lasted, with some alterations to fittings and layout, for one hundred and thirty years from 1868 to 1997. The fifth, and current phase, involved a re-orientation of the interior of the church to the original east west axis. This had the effect of restoring its initial classical orientation. Extra ground was acquired to the west of the original site and a 3,500 square feet parish centre was built adjacent to the west-side of the original building. As part of the project a time capsule of contemporary items and memorabilia was provided by various parishioners. This capsule will be opened in 2021. The images of the floor plan for St Andrew's for each of these phases were prepared by Donald Cromer whose family have been associated with St Andrew's almost from the time of its first construction.

The history of each phase and the architectural and decor issues and design philosophies underlying each phase are set out below.

Phase 1 – 1823 – The original layout - the first classical phase

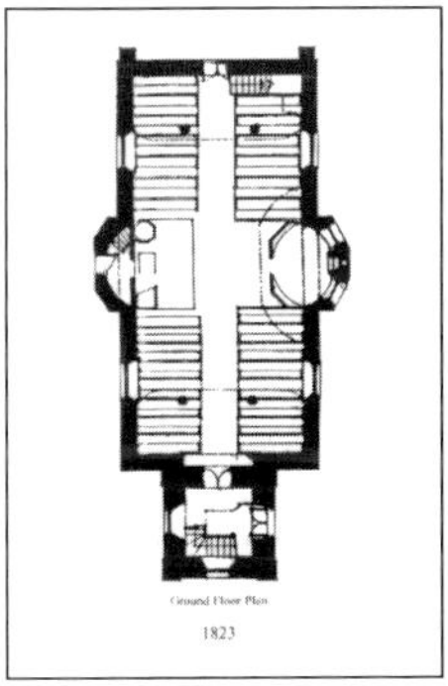

Plate 11: Floor Plan 1823 – Don Cromer Architects

St Andrew's site has a strong north south axis. However it was not sufficiently large to construct a church with the standard east west orientation for the longer axis of the nave. The original plan of St Andrews accommodated this physical restriction by use of a cross-axial internal layout to retain the east-facing window in the sanctuary area with an apse on the middle of the east side and a matching apse on the west side. Two balconies, each supported by two columns and faced in raised and fielded panelling, were inserted one each at the north and the south walls. The north balcony remains in place but the south balcony was removed in the mid-nineteenth century. The insertion of the balconies and the cross-axial plan accounts for the high ceiling of twenty-five feet in such a relatively modest space - the hall measures sixty feet by twenty seven feet. The ceiling consists of a flat plastered centre surrounded by narrow moulding and a shallow cove with a moulded cornice that circumvents the entire space. The columns supporting the balconies and the symmetry of the facing of the balconies and their arched doorways, box pews and the vaulted ceiling would have given the interior a very classical late eighteenth century feeling and an overall sense of coherence and unity.

The original building had four entrances, three for the congregation (tower, west wall and south wall) and one for the clergy on the east wall. The original window

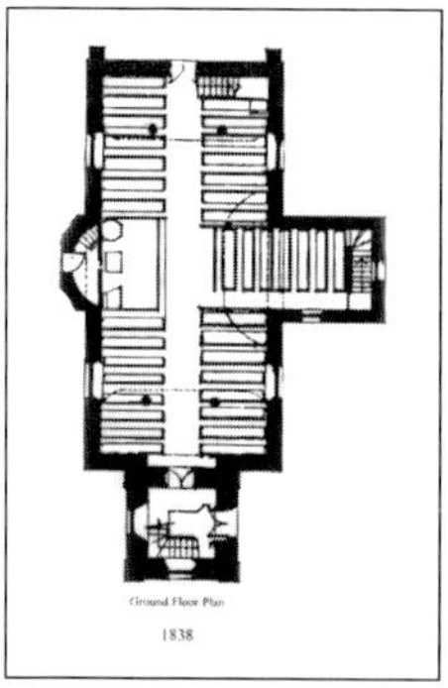

Plate 12: Floor Plan 1838 – Don Cromer Architects

layout consisted of three windows on the east and the west walls with two windows to the tower over the north balcony. It is likely that there were one or more windows on the south wall. The windows are made up of curvilinear tracery and diamond shaped panes. The original apse probably contained a solid reredos behind which was a small robing room with an external doorway. The original pews were high-sided box type pews. They are made of pine and were most likely made locally.

Phase 2 – 1840 to 1868 – The second classical phase - insertion of a third balcony and west transept

Only twenty years after St Andrew's was built the west apse was demolished and a small narrow transept, within

Plate 13: Internal layout of St Andrew's Church 2007

the original arch with tiered seating was inserted. A third balcony on the west wall in front of the new transept was also inserted at this time. These alterations were presumably made to increase the capacity of the church.

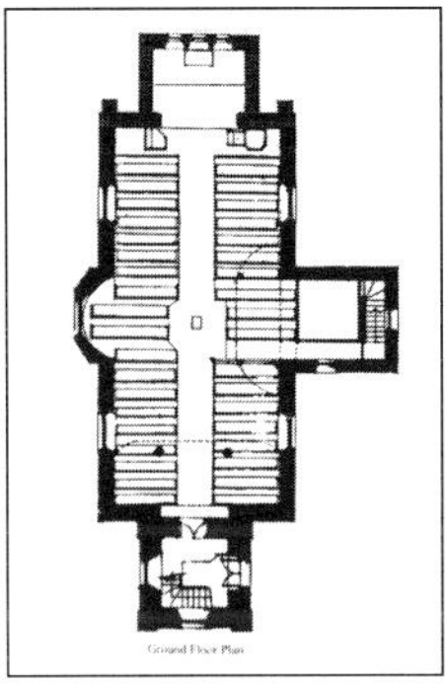

Plate 14: Floor Plan 1870 – Don Cromer Architects

Phase 3 – 1868 to 1960 – Creating a Victorian layout – removal of cross-axial orientation

Given the changing ecclesiastical views in the mid nineteenth century the results of the second phase may have been viewed by parishioners as old fashioned and less than satisfactory. Consequently only thirty years later in 1868 a radical new plan was proposed. Details of the new plan were submitted to and approved by the Ecclesiastical Commissioners. In the new layout the south and west balconies were demolished, an arch was inserted in the south gable and a modest sanctuary/chancel extension with a three light window was built. Stained glass was installed in the new south window and ceramic tiles were laid in the new chancel area. Most significantly the orientation of the pews was altered to face the new chancel, thereby giving the church a more common rectangular form. The pews themselves were retained, but cut down to a more bench like appearance. The resulting internal orientation was to the south, with a tendency to the east. The pulpit and prayer desk were moved to either side of the new sanctuary arch and wooden communion rails were installed. A biblical text was inscribed over the new arch. The west transept was converted into a robing and vestry room – fronted by the organ in the

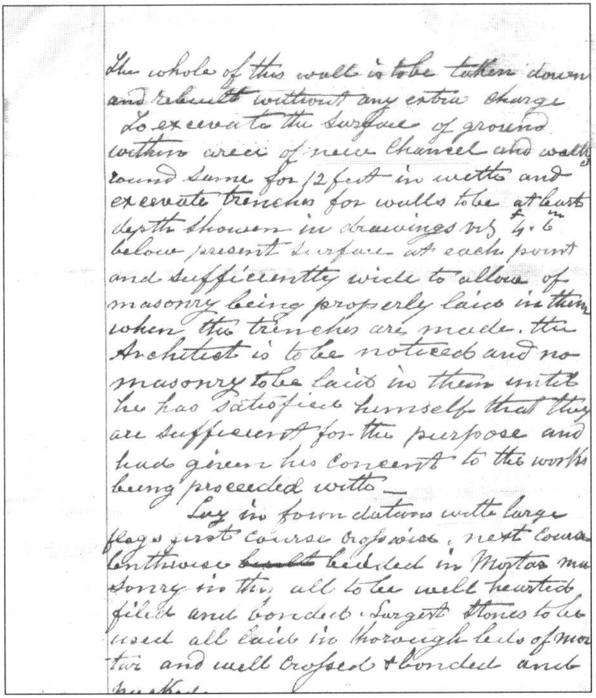

The whole of this wall is to be taken down
and rebuilt without any extra charge
To excavate the surface of ground
within area of new Chancel and walls
round same for 12 feet in width and
excavate trenches for walls to be at least
depth shown in drawings viz 4 ft 6 in
below present surface at each point
and sufficiently wide to allow of
masonry being properly laid in them
when the trenches are made. the
Architect is to be noticed and no
masonry to be laid in them until
he has satisfied himself that they
are sufficient for the purpose and
had given his consent to the works
being proceeded with –
Lay in foundations with large
flags first course crosswise, next course
lengthwise ~~built~~ bedded in Mortar ma-
sonry in this, all to be well hearted
filled and bonded. Largest stones to be
used all laid in thorough beds of mor-
tar and well crossed + bonded and
[illegible]

Plate 15: Part of alteration request to RCB 1868

1890s. St Andrew's retained this basic layout for the next 130 years although numerous minor changes occurred from time to time. These later changes included the insertion of a baptismal font in the middle of the aisle, alterations to the pews and the re-location of the memorial wall tablets from the south gable to the walls in the north balcony. Later changes included the insertion of the centenary stained glass window in 1923 in the eastern apse, and the adjoining Cromer window also in 1923. A major new heating system was installed in the late 1880's.

Phase 4 –1960 - Modernisation and refurbishment

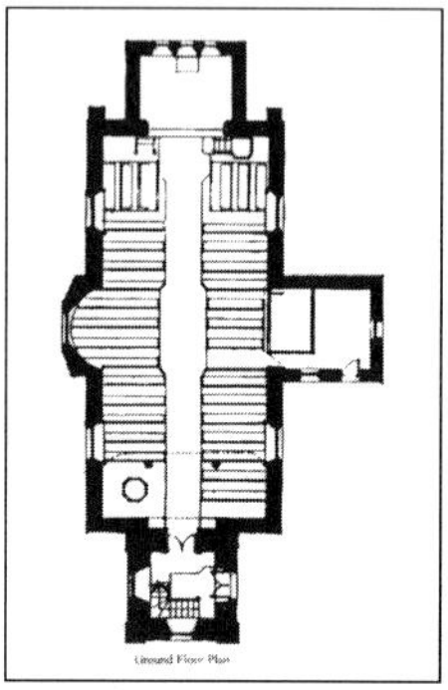

Plate 16: Floor plan 1960 – Don Cromer Architects

Despite the constant attention paid to the maintenance of the building by the select vestry, St Andrew's required major renovations by 1960. The work was supervised by J. D. Featherstone and it was undertaken by Mr R. Syme, who was a parishioner. Changes from this time included moving the baptismal font to the rear of the church and changes to the layout of the choir, pulpit and sanctuary furniture. The text on the south arch was over-painted, carpet was installed and the entire building was redecorated. Over time both the select vestries of parishes and the central authorities within the Church of Ireland began to recognise the architectural and historical importance of its building stock. In the case of St Andrew's this is evidenced by the involvement of the RCB architects in later development phases - for example at the April 1949 vestry meeting William Cromer recommended that the parish should consult with the RCB architect Mr Murphy regarding the works being undertaken. This process of regular consultation still continues.[26] The Cromer family involvement with both of the churches in Leixlip Union parish stretches back to the middle of the nineteenth century, continuing to this day through Donald Cromer, son of the William Cromer mentioned above. Donald Cromer is currently the architect for Leixlip Union parish and was the architect for the construction of the parish centre and the re-orientation of the church carried out in 1997. He is also the architect for the major conservation and development project currently being carried out in St Mary's, Leixlip.

Phase 5 – 1995 – Construction of the parish centre and re-instatement of the classical cross-axial orientation

In 1995 the Select Vestry launched a major development project in St Andrew's. A parcel of land to the west of the original site was acquired from the neighbouring garden and a smaller piece to the south of the original site. In a bold piece of architecture designed by Donald Cromer, a parish centre complete with badminton/bowling hall and stage, a kitchen, three toilets and a meeting room was built. The new building has a sun patio to the rear and is fully wheelchair accessible. A 'Quiet Room', which can also be used as an extension to the seating in the church, was inserted at the ground level of the link between the original transept and the new building. On the first floor of the link section two offices for parish administrative staff and the rector were installed. The new building was set a metre lower than the floor level of the original building and faced in grey Leinster limestone calp. The combination of a matching stone facing and low roof when sited alongside the existing wall presents a unified yet unimposing structure.

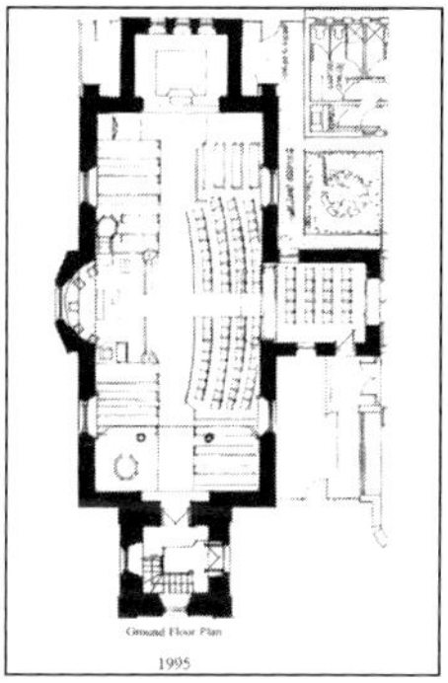

Plate 17: Floor Plan 1995 – Don Cromer Architects

Inside the church the original internal cross-axial layout was restored and the pews at the north and south end were re-oriented to face one another with a set of pews in the centre facing the raised dais for the holy table, pulpit, sanctuary chairs, prayer desks and the centenary window. The floor was set in concrete thereby removing the last vestiges of the troublesome late nineteenth century heating system. The original pews were used in the new layout. The colour scheme - pale blue walls, together with white woodwork and ceiling, and pale antique pine pews - aimed to reflect the late georgian neo-classical character of the original layout. This major project was financed by a combination of asset sales, fundraising, grants, donations and borrowing.

St Andrew's Lucan - maintaining the fabric

As noted earlier, parish churches are in many respects a memorial to the generations of parishioners who have cared for and maintained the building and its environment. The archives in the RCBL contain many documents that allow us to trace the maintenance activities in St Andrew's since 1823. Central to this story are the vestry minutes which are available from 1822 onwards, the sets of printed and hand written accounts for most years from 1888 to 1910, and other documents including drawings of the interior of St Andrew's. Interestingly the minutes invariably refer to Lucan Church or the church in Lucan and almost never by its full name of St Andrew's. In all of these documents there are frequent references to parishioners' concerns in respect of the condition of the church, listings of the details of expenditure on repairs to windows, roof, doors, heating etc. and also to preventative maintenance by cleaning the gutters. In addition the walls and grounds

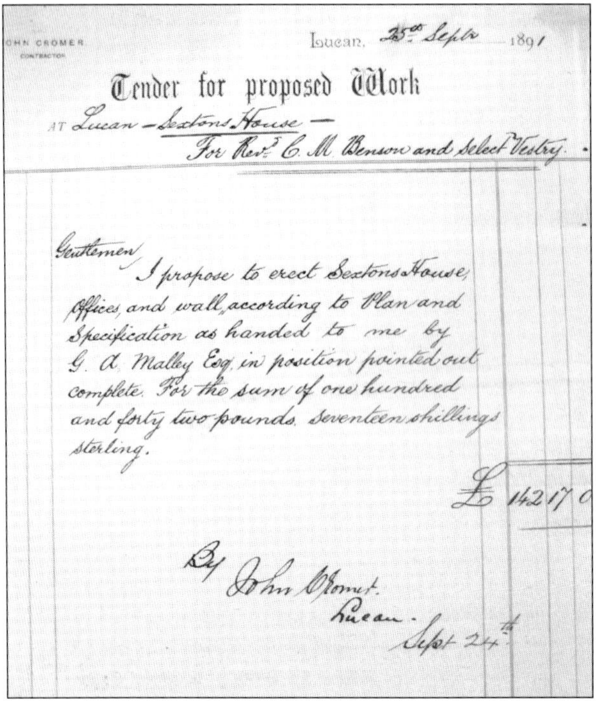
OHN CROMER
CONTRACTOR

Lucan, 25th Sept 1891

Tender for proposed Work

AT Lucan — Sextons House —
For Revd C. M. Benson and Select Vestry.

Gentlemen
I propose to erect Sextons House, Offices, and wall, according to Plan and Specification as handed to me by G. A. Malley Esq. in position pointed out complete. For the sum of one hundred and forty two pounds, seventeen shillings sterling.

£ 142 17 0

By John Cromer.
Lucan.
Sept 24th

Plate 18: Example of works estimate from John Cromer – RCBL P.0913

of the church also called for constant care and maintenance – viz. drainage, tree pruning and management of the surface in the churchyard.

It would be tedious to list all of the maintenance items mentioned in the minutes over such a long period. However, selected examples from a variety of periods which reflect the never ending battle to maintain fabric using the limited resources available in a voluntary situation are set out below. For example, in 1888 'Repairs to Lead lights, Windows, and other church matter' cost £1 13s. 2d. In the next year 'Repairs, Church Railings' cost 11s. The stove was repaired at a cost of 17s. in 1892 (see below for further details on the fifteen year saga of the heating system in the period from 1888 to early in the new century). A lamp was bought and one was repaired in 1894. The church bell was fixed in 1895, as was the lock to the door and gravel to the value of 3s. 6d. was bought for the churchyard. Other maintenance items included 'cutting ivy and clearing gutters' at a cost of 2s. in 1900. Gibson and Sons were paid £13 16s. 4d. in 1897 for painting. External painting cost £13 in 1902 and in that year the accounts give an unusually detailed breakdown of John Cromer's bill for Wind Guards £5, Ladder £1 15s. 0d. Repairing Ladder Shelter £1 0s. 0d., Chancel Gutters £0 5s. 0d. and Sundry repairs to Church £2 14s. 0d. coming to a total cost of £10 14s. 0d.

Financing such expenditure was a constant source of concern for the vestry. As today the sources of finance varied. Relatively minor expenditure for regular maintenance was paid from parish income, however, where more significant expenditure was required, the practise was to establish a special fund and to raise the required finance either by appeals to parishioners or by requests to the Ecclesiastical Commissioners and post dis-establishment of the Church of Ireland in 1870 from the RCB. Throughout the nineteenth century the property portfolio of the parish in Lucan consisted not just of St Andrew's but also the schoolhouse across the road from 1827, a schoolmaster's house from 1872, a Glebe house from 1825 and a sextons house from 1872. The maintenance of the fabric of this portfolio of buildings was the dominant theme of the vestry meetings throughout this period. The constant battle to raise the finance for such regular repairs is well illustrated by the discussion at the vestry re painting and cleaning from February 1889. There was apparently some dissension among the members of the vestry, who finally passed a resolution that 'the matter of a thorough painting & cleaning Lucan church be deferred for the present, or until the necessity for such painting & cleaning become more apparent.' At the next meeting the appointed committee reported that Mr Gibson of Mary Street in Dublin had inspected the church and forwarded a specification which they recommended. As for subscriptions it was felt that with £10 already paid and promises of £21 more without any request being made the vestry felt confident to proceed.[27]

Each year brought new maintenance and development issues. In January 1901 a letter from Mr Browne re 'drainage of the space in front of the church' was discussed but no action taken.[28] The meeting of 25 October 1925 noted that 'the desirability of lopping off some branches of the trees which were hiding the view of Lucan Church clock which had recently been painted'. Some years later in October 1941 Mr Cromer bought the trees for £5 and removed them and provided some of the cuttings as fuel for the heating of the church. The next meeting noted the improvement in the appearance of the church grounds. Electric lighting was installed in 1935 at a cost of £50 but unforeseen costs associated with this and some redecorating amounted to £55 which the rector sought from the Beresford Fund.[29] The steeple required approximately £40/50 of work in 1936 and the wall needed circa £72 of work in 1940. However as no funds were available, Mr R. Magahy 'suggested that if the matter was left to him for the present he would see what might be done'. In April 1949 William Cromer suggested that the front door should be replaced but parish funds were not available at the time. In April 1950 he suggested that if the vestry paid for the materials he would make the door. Later in October 1950 he was thanked for the erection of the entrance door. William Cromer reported on the roof and belfry in 1955 and gave a comprehensive report of various costs totalling £610 to the July meeting. These issues were addressed by the major work carried out in 1960. Like any public building there is a risk of vandalism, for example the meeting of 24th January 1894 resolved 'That a reward of £1 be offered for such information as would lead to the conviction of the person or persons who broke one of the east windows of the parish church of Lucan between Sunday 21st Jan and Wednesday 24th Jan 1894.'[30]

This pattern of minor and major maintenance continues to this day – for example in the last seven years the parish has spent maintenance money on the roof in 2004, on the drains in 2005, repainted the parish centre in 2005 and, as outlined below, the time has come for a full re-decoration of the church which will be carried out over the next few years.

A related aspect of fabric management that received regular attention by the vestry was the appropriate level of insurance that should be maintained on parish property. For example at the January 1891 meeting it was decided to 'insure the church furniture for £50, leaving a sum of £1400 re the buildings etc'. The total value of the insurance was £1,760 including windows.[31]

INTERNAL ARTWORKS AND FITTINGS IN ST ANDREW'S

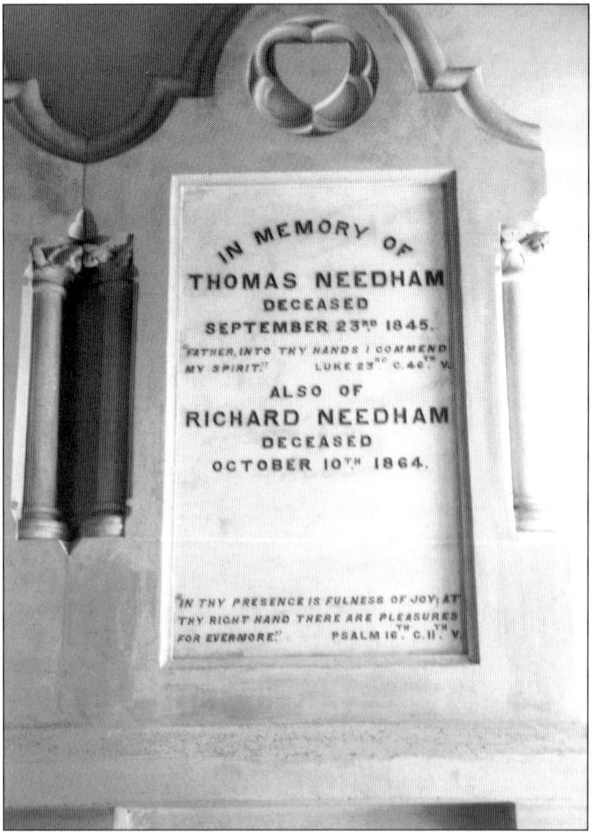

Plate 19: Part of the Needham monument St Andrew's Church Lucan

A description of the architectural features and evolution is only one part of the story of a church. The other part consists of the internal fittings, artworks and materials. Stone and brass memorials and plaques commemorating the donation of particular items of furniture by family members in memory of deceased relatives or in honour of long serving rectors, vestry persons or parishioners are a common feature of most Church of Ireland parish churches. In this tradition St Andrew's has seven stone memorials and also a number of other dedicated items (windows, furniture etc).

The seven stone panels in St Andrew's are now located on the three walls of the north gallery and they commemorate a total of nineteen named individuals. The memorials are to various members of the Vesey and Colthurst family of Lucan House (five memorials), the Needhams of Edmundsburry (a triptych) and a single memorial to the Scott family of Woodville House. The presence of the Vesey and Needham family memorials is understandable given their leadership of the parish at the time of the construction of St Andrew's in the early 1820s. All of these stone monuments date from the nineteenth century.

The vestry minutes record the events surrounding the erection of some of these memorials. In addition to these monuments there is a single slab in the entrance porch commemorating the long service of Revd Henry Stewart to Leixlip Union. The text simply reads 'In Memoriam, C V Henry Stewart 1874'. The text of the seven stone memorials is set out overleaf.

As in any organisation, and perhaps particularly in the case of voluntary ones, the story behind the erection of monuments in Church of Ireland churches is never an easy one. There are differing and sometimes strongly held views on the appropriateness of such monuments in the first place, secondly the qualification criteria for being honoured by such a memorial and lastly on issues of cost and style. St Andrew's is no exception to this general pattern. For example, on 5 September 1888 at a vestry meeting attended by only six vestrymen, (all were regular members of the vestry) and chaired by R. E. Gibson in the absence of the incumbent, the vestry refused (on the casting vote of the chairman) to adjourn the meeting so that a larger attendance could be secured to approve a motion that a 'subscription list be opened for the purpose of erecting a memorial to the late Colonel Vesey.' At the same meeting a second motion, this time carried by the casting vote of the chairman, was passed which stated that 'Mrs Vesey's application for permission to erect a tablet in the wall of her gallery pew to the memory of the late Colonel Vesey be granted.' A third motion proposed that on the return of the incumbent, a meeting of the vestry to consider a motion to open a subscription and to consider what type of memorial would meet with Mrs Vesey's approval was passed unanimously, as was a fourth motion to the effect that no fees should be charged for the erection of such a monument. Notwithstanding the contradictory nature of the above series of motions, Mrs Vesey was immediately informed of the decision of the select vestry and her letter of reply, accepting the offer to allow a tablet to be erected, dated the next day 6 September 1888 was read into the record at the next vestry meeting on 24 October 1888.

The October meeting was attended by the incumbent C.M. Benson and nine vestrymen. Given Mrs Vesey's acceptance of permission to proceed it was agreed that the 'select vestry consider it inadvisable to take any further steps in relation to the proposed mural memorial.' In her letter Mrs Vesey had noted that she understood that 'there was some dislike to the idea (not I know from any personal motive) but on other grounds in which I myself agree as I think them [tablets] as a rule disfiguring and undesirable.'

In memory of Mary the wife of Thomas Richard Needham deceased March 7th. 1853. "To live in Christ to die is gain" Philippians 1sr c 21st v. also of his sisters Rachael Needham deceased 12th February 1871 and Caroline Needham deceased 13th October 1871 and also of the above Thomas Richard Needham deceased 4th February 1872. "Death is swallowed up in victory" 1sr. Cor.15th, c.54thv.

In memory of Charlotte Matilda wife of Captain Henry Needham deceased October 27th 1854. "Today shalt thou be with me in paradise" Luke 23rd, c. 43rd V. "God hath given to us eternal life and this life is his son" 1. John 5th, c. 11th v.

In memory of Thomas Needham deceased September 12rd 1845. "Father into thy hands I commend My spirit" Luke 12rd, c. 44th . v. Also of Richard Needham deceased October 10th 1864. "In thy presence is fullness of joy; at thy right hand there are pleasures for evermore" Psalm 16th. C. 11th.V.

Sacred to the memory of Gen. Sir Hopton Stratford Scott K.C.B. A brave and determined officer in the H.E.I.C.S. for more than thirty years. He died at Woodville Lucan on 23rrd June 1860. Most sincerely regretted by all who knew him also to Mary Anna Scott. Who died June 28th 1845. Arthur Stratford Scott. Who died Jan. 4th 1831. Reginald Baliol Scott. Who died April 2nd 1841. Children of the above. Also to Mary Davie Scott wife of the above who died at Woodville March 13th 1867. "Her children rise up and call her blessed; her husband also, and he praiseth her." Prov.Ch.31 Vers.28. "Blessed are the dead which die in the lord. Yea, saith the spirit, that they may rest from their labours; and their works do follow them." Rev. 14.13 v.

Elizabeth daughter of the late George Vesey Esq. and relict of the late Sir Nicholas Conway Colthurst Bart. Departed this life on the 12th day of November 1840 aged 48. Looking for that blessed hope and the glorious appearing of the great lord and our saviour Jesus Christ

In loving memory of Charles Colthurst Vesey who on the 11th of may 1885 entered into rest aged 58 years. "And I shall five unto them eternal rest and they shall never perish." John X. 28.

Sacred to the memory of George Vesey who on the 11th of April 1836 in the 75th year of his age departed this life. "Looking unto Jesus the author and finisher of our faith" Hebrews

To the beloved memory of George Colthurst Vesey Capt. 1st. Shropshire L.I. Eldest son of the late Col. Colthurst Vesey died at Hong Kong 4th. June 1894 at the post of duty aged 35. "Waiting for the coming of our Lord Jesus Christ."

Sacred to the memory of Emily Vesey relict of the late George Vesey who on the 12th. Of January 1854 in the 87th. year of her age departed this life. When Christ who is our life shall appear, then shall ye also appear with him in Glory. Colossians mch. Ivv.

She went on to state that 'It has, however been a habit in the family, & I was willing since my dear husband's tomb is out of sight, that his name should be absent from the mural record for those who come after him.' She also expressed a view that she was against subscriptions as 'I fear it entails a tax on others, which he would have been the last to wish'. Only six years later in August 1894 a resolution re the erection of a tablet to the memory of George C. Vesey was passed without any apparent controversy. A resolution to erect a lectern in his memory and to open a subscription fund was also passed at the same meeting. Costs were estimated to be circa £40 and Mr R. G. Nash was 'requested to inspect some of the English works to obtain the best net price' on a forthcoming private visit to London. Both tablets are now located on the walls of the gallery in St Andrew's.[32]

Some years later, perhaps feeling that the church had a sufficiency of such tablets, a request from Revd D.V. O'Meara in January 1922 to erect 'a brass or marble mural tablet on the east wall of the interior of the church in memory of certain members of the Thornbury family of which his wife was a member' was rejected with the comment that it was 'undesirable that any mural tablet be placed in the body of the church.'[33]

Plate 20: Donated church furniture St Andrew's Lucan

As is usual in churches, many of the furnishings were either donated by, or financed by parishioners in memory of family members. Among the items in St Andrew's which have specific dedications are the Holy Table which is in memory of Ruth Whiteside, presented by her husband and family, the baptismal font erected in memory of Revd Henry Stewart in 1874, the credence table in memory of Robert Magahy and his son Charles who were the organists in St Andrew's for seventy eight years from 1882 to 1959, the prayer desks in memory of John Cromer (donated by his wife Gladys, daughter Lillian and son John) and the hymn board in memory of Hamilton Thonburry (died 1885).[34]

The tradition of dedicating items of furniture continues today, and in 2007 two new chairs, decorated with a St Andrew's cross, were purchased for the sanctuary area from funds donated by St Mary's Roman Catholic church Lucan in thanks for the period in 2005 when St Andrew's was used by the parishioners of St Mary's while that church was undergoing one of its regular transformation projects.

In November 1911 the vestry resolved that brass communion rails be erected in place of the wooden ones and dedicated to the long serving incumbent C. M. Benson (1871-1911).[35] The plaque reads 'These communion rails were erected by the wish of Rev. C. M. Benson M.A. out of funds subscribed by the parishioners and other friends on the occasion of his resignation July 1911 as a small tribute to his long and faithful services as incumbent to this parish (1871-1911).'

A pipe organ was installed in St Andrew's in the late nineteenth century. In November 1881 it was resolved that 'the ladies of the parish be respectfully invited to form themselves into a committee for the purpose of collection of the funds necessary to purchase the proposed organ by means of a bazaar or otherwise'.[36] A subscription fund of £204. 5s. was raised and the organ was purchased from Peter Conacher & Co., Springwood Huddersfield. The organ is two-manual, with five stops on the Great organ and six on the Swell. It has the usual manual and pedal couplers and one pedal stop (Bourdon). By their nature, as complex mechanical structures' pipe organs need regular maintenance and servicing. Following the installation of the organ these costs became a regular feature of the parish accounts. For example on 30th November 1948 two estimates, one for cleaning the organ for £52 and one for installing an electric blower for £80 were submitted for consideration. This work was duly carried out and it was partly funded by the legacy of Miss Bellamy.[37]

Stained glass is another favoured form of memorial in churches of all denominations. There are three such windows in St Andrew's. The first was installed in the sanctuary during the 1868 renovations. The dedication reads 'Erected by his sorrowing wife in loving remembrance of Thomas Purefoy M.D. which died Decr. 23rd 1868 – I have waited for thy salvation O Lord'.' In March 1922 the vestry addressed the issue of the appropriate means 'if any' to mark the centenary of the

Lucan Organ Fund, 1882.

	£ s. d.	£ s. d.
Mr. Stanford (including £4 5s. extra expenses of new Vestry and Organ Chamber)		34 5 0
Rev. C. M. Benson	15 0 0	
Per same—Sale of Picture by Miss C. E. Benson ...	3 10 0	
" Mrs. Rohde	2 2 0	
" Mrs. Benson, sen. and Miss Benson	2 0 0	
" Mr. J. Harrison	1 0 0	
" Mrs. G. V. Benson ...	0 10 0	
" Dr. and Mrs. A. Barker ...	0 10 0	
" Mrs. Bass	0 2 6	
" Miss Hall	0 2 6—	24 17 0
Colonel Vesey		15 0 0
Mr. R. E. Gibson	4 0 0	
Per same—Lord Essex	5 0 0	
" Miss Clarke	3 0 0	
" Mr. Mayne	1 1 0—	13 1 0
Mrs. Vesey	8 0 0	
Per same—Hon. Mrs. Handcock ...	2 0 0	
" Mrs. Hartley	1 0 0	
" Mrs. Warren	1 0 0—	12 0 0
Mrs. Stanford	5 0 0	
Per same—Mrs. Stanford, senr. ...	2 0 0	
" Rev. W. Kynnaston ...	1 0 0	
" Dr. White	1 0 0	
" Miss Reid	0 10 0	
" Mrs. Scott	0 10 0	
" Small sums	0 8 0	
" Mrs. Stanford's Servants	0 6 0	
" Mrs. Flanigan	0 5 0	
" Rev. T. A. Holcroft ...	0 5 0	
" Mr. Johnston (Clonsilla)	0 5 0	
" Mr. J. M'Donald ...	0 1 0—	11 10 0
Anonymous		11 0 0
Mr. Dunlop	5 0 0	
Per same—Mr. Cathcart	0 10 0	
" Mr. More	0 10 0—	6 0 0
Mr. Bellaney		5 0 0
Mrs. Moran		5 0 0
Miss L. C. Stubbs	1 5 6	
Per same—Miss Phelan	1 11 6	
" Mrs. Colley	0 15 0	
" Mrs. Fitzgerald ...	0 10 0	
" A Friend	0 5 0	
" Miss A. Beale	0 2 6	
" Miss A. Glascott ...	0 2 6	
" Miss R. C. Morgan ...	0 2 6	
" Mr. A. Stubbs	0 2 6	
" Miss M. Usher	0 2 0	
" Mrs. Russell	0 1 0—	5 0 0
Mr. Wills		5 0 0
Per Mrs. Nuttall—Captain H. Baker ...	1 5 0	
" Mrs. Harrison	1 0 0	

	£ s. d.	£ s. d.
Per Mrs Nuttall—Mr. A. Frost	0 10 0	
" Mrs. Reid	0 10 0	
" Mr. J. Revell	0 10 0	
" Mrs. Rowlands	0 5	
" Mrs. Atkinson	0 2 6	
" Mrs. Stoney	0 2 6	4 5 0
Mr. Clarke		4 0 0
Mr. J. Cromer	1 0 0	
Per same—Mrs. J. Cromer	1 0 0	
" Mr. Cromer's Family ...	1 0 0—	3 0 0
Dr. Levinge		3 0 0
Mr. James W. Hill		2 2 0
Mr. James Gibson		2 0 0
Mr. W. Smith		2 0 0
Mr. A. M'Clelland		1 5 0
Miss Maud Gibson (collected)		1 0 0
Mr. T. Johnson		1 0 0
Mr. W. Palmer		1 0 0
Mr. W. Pinkerton		1 0 0
Mr. W. Thornbury		1 0 0
Miss Cahusac		0 15 0
Mr. T. Poole		0 15 0
Mrs. Ainsley		0 10 0
Anonymous		0 10 0
Mr. S. Buckley		0 10 0
Mrs. Chandlee		0 10 0
Mrs. Dunlop, senior		0 10 0
Mr. Eastwood		0 10 0
Mr. Proctor		0 10 0
Mrs Rainsford		0 10 0
Mr. C. Armstrong		0 5 0
Mr. J. F. Cole		0 5 0
Mr. T. Cromer		0 5 0
Mrs. Magrath		0 5 0
Mr. M'Donell		0 5 0
Mr. and Mrs. Fegan		0 5 0
Mr. Gray		0 5 0
Miss Nuttall		0 5 0
Mr. Lowry		0 4 0
Mr. Flanigan		0 2 6
Mr. Loftus		0 2 6
Mr. Magahy		0 2 6
Mr. William Nicholson		0 2 6
Mr. Stanton		0 2 6
Miss Young		0 2 6
Mr. Andrews		0 2 0
Mr. Cane		0 2 0
Mr. N. Nicholson		0 2 0
Proceeds of Choral Union Concert, December 1881		2 8 10
Offertory—Ascension Day 1882...		7 8 8
"Found"		0 2 8
Interest on lodgments in Post Office Savings' Bank		0 4 4
Harvest Festival—Part Offertory		11 0 6
Total cost of Organ and Chamber		**£204 5 0**

Plate 21: Organ subscription list 1882 – RCBL P.0913

Plate 22: Organ St Andrew's Lucan 2007

foundation of the church. At the meeting of 16 October 1923 'a suggestion was put forward by Msrs Cromer and Harrison that a stained glass window should be erected met with approval'. Ideas for designs which had already been secured from the firm of Ward & Partners in Belfast were discussed and it was agreed that the rector would consult with Mrs Purser's firm in Dublin. At the meeting of 30 October it was noted that 'Mrs Purser had inspected the proposed site of the centenary memorial window and had submitted a design which met with general approval – she would erect this window at a cost of £100.' The window was to be 'erected opposite the organ.' The window depicts Christ as the good shepherd, which is also the image associated with St Andrew. The work proceeded immediately and a dedication and commemorative service was held on Friday 7 December. This was the anniversary of the dedication of the church, and the sermon was preached by the Archbishop of Dublin. Sarah Purser's firm An Tur Gloinne, 'The Glass Tower' was one of the two main stained glass studios in this period, the workshop of Harry Clarke being the other. Dr Peter Harbison the leading art historian has described the quality of the work produced by these studios to meet the demand of a large number of both Church of Ireland and Roman Catholic commissions as 'Ireland's greatest gift to European twentieth century art'. We are fortunate in Lucan to be the custodians of such a heritage.

On 11 November 1924 'formal permission of the vestry was granted to Mr John Cromer to erect a stained glass window at the upper east side of the church in memory of his sister the late Miss Mary Cromer' and at the next meeting John Cromer submitted a design from Powells of London. The window was dedicated by the rector Rev. Gillman at the Easter Sunday service in 1925. The text on the window reads 'To the Glory of God and in loving memory of Mary Cromer who entered into rest 14 July 1923 aged 54. This window has been erected by her brother John Cromer. "Their works do follow them"'. One immediate consequence was the need to 'increase the insurance on the stained glass windows in Lucan Church by £400.'

Plate 23: 1923 Good Shepherd Centenary window

In February 1881 the 'question of heating the church with hot water pipes' was considered and an estimate for the work of £93 from Roe & Murray was submitted to the meeting. It was decided to call a meeting of the select vestry for 4.30 p.m. on Saturday Feb 26th to consider the whole matter. At this meeting a number of other quotes were considered but it was 'decided to do nothing in the matter at present.'[39] These meetings however were the beginning of a lengthy correspondence on this issue between Revd Benson and various equipment suppliers, suppliers of testimonials and contractors. The RCBL archive contains a separate nearly one-inch thick file of these letters stretching from 1881 to the early years of the new century. Other initial estimates from 1881 were Stanford's in Dawson Street, outlining that the system would cost 'at least fifty pounds' and one from Thomas Henshaw & Co. in Middle Abbey Street of '£40 to £50'. The project was not proceeded with at that time partly for financial reasons, and also because of a debate over the most effective method of heating the church – water or air. Finally in 1888 John Grundy of London proposed to supply and install the equipment (net of construction work) for his patented 'Pure warm air' system for the sum of £35. In 1882 Grundy published a sixty page testimonial booklet listing several hundred - principally church but also some domestic testimonials - to the effectiveness of his system. The

Plate 24: 1923 Cromer window St Andrew's Lucan

testimonials included eight from Dublin which included the Dublin Fever Hospital, and one from Sir Thomas Drew, a leading Dublin Architect. The issue was raised again in 1897 and further letters of clarification ensued. Finally on 8 June 1897 it was agreed that 'Grundy's hot air system of heating be introduced in to 'Lucan Church'. A committee was appointed with a budget of £60 to agree the specifications.

Work proceeded, and in December 1897 the balance of £30 due to Mr Grundy was to be released 'when the apparatus shall be made to work to the satisfaction of the committee.' As implied by the above comment the installation did not go smoothly. For example in July 1887 Grundy professed himself disappointed that 'Hunt (the installation contractor) should be too lazy to whitewash the chamber in preference to wasting time until the apparatus got up. He charged me with full time which is 70 hours to the week – viz. 12 each day except Sat 10 being charged that day'. However, despite several other interventions from Grundy this was not the end of the matter, and in May 1898 Grundy expressed his sorrow to find 'there is yet cause for dissatisfaction and this ought not to be the case'. Intermittent correspondence continued thereafter, and as late as June 1902 it was noted that 'After considerable discussion, and the reading of a letter addressed to the churchwardens signed by several ladies complaining of the present heating & ventilation of the church' it was agreed to investigate the use of a 'central ventilation in the roof'. However this did

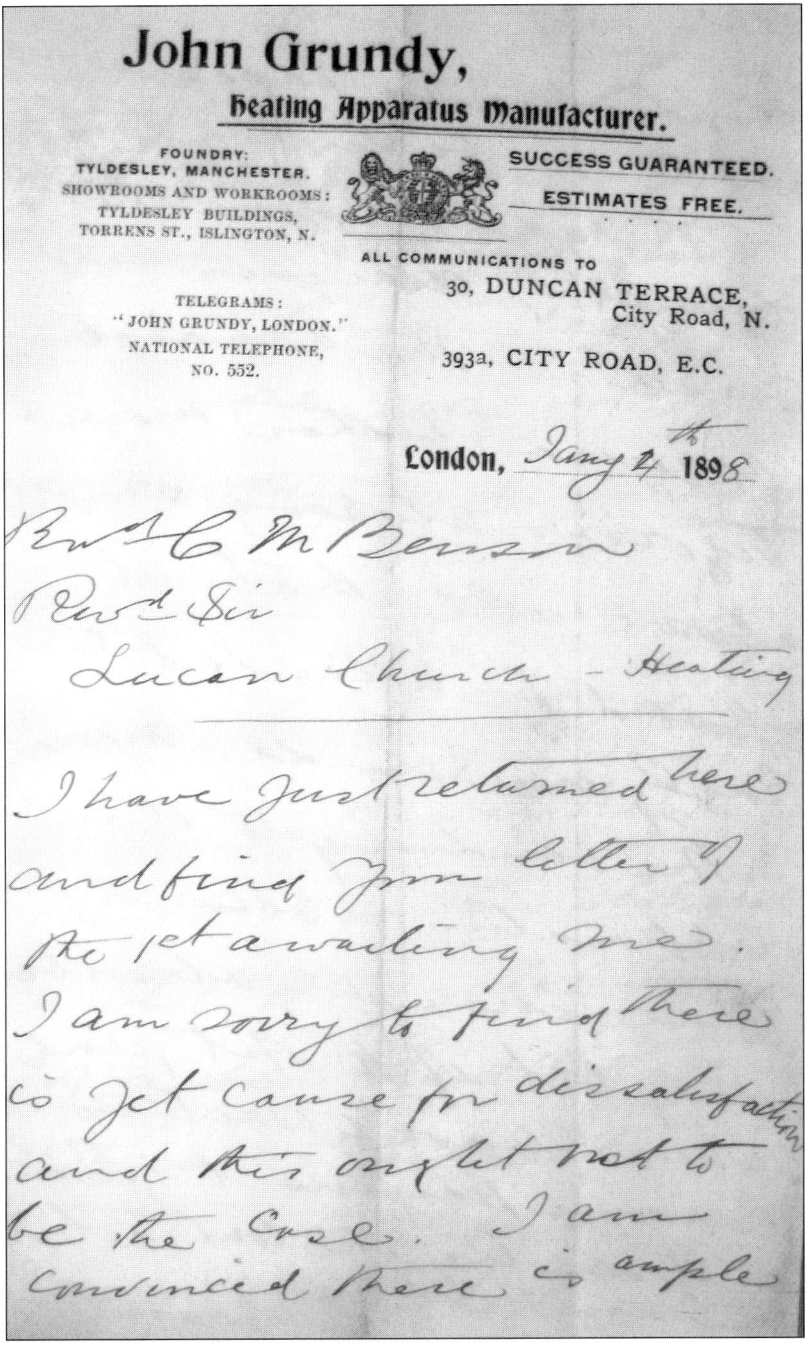

John Grundy,

Heating Apparatus Manufacturer.

FOUNDRY:
TYLDESLEY, MANCHESTER.
SHOWROOMS AND WORKROOMS:
TYLDESLEY BUILDINGS,
TORRENS ST., ISLINGTON, N.

SUCCESS GUARANTEED.

ESTIMATES FREE.

ALL COMMUNICATIONS TO
30, DUNCAN TERRACE,
City Road, N.

393a, CITY ROAD, E.C.

TELEGRAMS:
"JOHN GRUNDY, LONDON."
NATIONAL TELEPHONE,
NO. 552.

London, Jany 4th 1898

Revd C M Benson

Revd Sir

Lucan Church - Heating

I have just returned here and find your letter of the 1st awaiting me. I am sorry to find there is yet cause for dissatisfaction and this ought not to be the case. I am convinced there is ample

Plate 25: Extract from Grundy correspondence – RCBL P.0913

not seem to be practical and it was agreed to see if the windows could be made to open 'from above downwards' as they 'apparently had once been capable' and following various discussion with John Cromer it was 'decided to try the effect of glass wind guards to each of the five side windows'. The functioning of, or rather the lack of a functioning heating system was still an issue for the vestry in January 1918.[40]

St Andrew's in the community

As already noted the vestry minutes are very focussed on the issues within its competence i.e. fabric maintenance for its building portfolio. Other issues such as major political events in the life of Lucan or of the country go almost completely unrecorded in the minutes of the vestry. One of the few examples noted was the impact of the First World War, when the vestry recorded expressions of condolences to families on the death of a number of parishioners. In a minute in January 1918 it was noted that 'The Rector mentioned that it had been suggested to remove a pew at the end of the church to admit of under seating accommodation for the soldier patients at Hermitage Auxiliary Hospital.' In May 1919 a discussion took place on the possibility of erecting a memorial 'in connection with parishioners who had fought in the war'. There is no later mention of this proposal and there is no such memorial in the church today.[41]

Today St Andrew's church and the Church of Ireland Parish Centre are an important religious and social focal point for the people of Lucan. Sunday service is attended by an average of over 150 parishioners and visitors each week. The centre hosts around fifty meetings, events, courses, classes and other activities weekly with as many one thousand people using the facilities. Other major social events at St Andrew's include the Christmas Fair, the Parish Pantomime, children's summer camp and the bi-annual People's Art Exhibition. In recent years St Andrew's has played an important interdenominational role in Lucan. In 2005 Mass was celebrated every Sunday for the parishioners of St Mary's in Lucan during the six month period when St Mary's was closed for renovations. Since 2005 an African based church has held their Sunday afternoon service in St Andrew's, with attendance in excess of one hundred persons. Members of the Muslim medical community have also used the parish centre for prayer on Fridays since 2006. These two recent visitors have certainly made a significant change from the tradition of Church of Ireland liturgy 'in the English Tounge.'

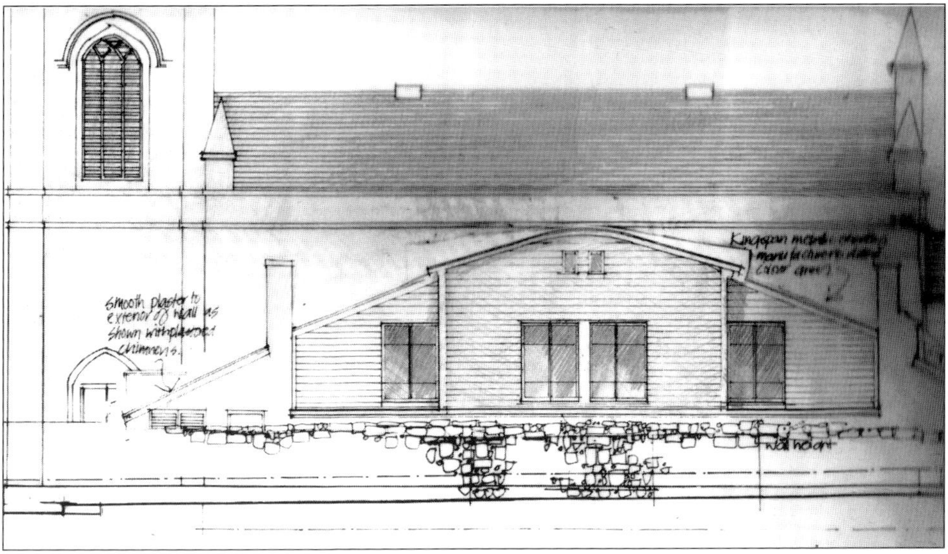

Figure 1: West elevation of parish centre and St Andrew's church – Don Cromer Architects

The future of St Andrew's

All church buildings undergo periodic transformations and upgrades to meet new needs and to upgrade facilities to meet the requirements of later ages. As noted above, this is in addition to the constant need for regular repair and maintenance. In the past the practice has often been that each renovation has led to the loss of much of the fabric and character inherited from the previous generation, resulting in immense value being lost. Modern practice is much more sensitive regarding the need to conserve both fabric and character of historic buildings. The challenge is which character do we conserve? In the case of St Andrew's is it the classical character of the original design or is it the Victorian character evident in St Andrew's for nearly one hundred and thirty years. Every generation wishes to make its mark but it is also the responsibility of each generation to maintain, conserve and where possible to develop the built heritage that is handed down to them from previous generations. The select vestry of Leixlip Union are fully cognisant of this onerous responsibility. The RCB is also cognisant of the wider heritage of the Church of Ireland and all historic buildings are now subject to a five yearly condition review. Recommendations are issued to select vestries on any necessary works identified as part of this review. While at this time there are no major transformational plans for St Andrew's, the work of ongoing maintenance will of course continue. In particular the select vestry is very aware that the bicentennial anniversary of the construction of St Andrew's is now only fifteen years hence and it is likely that some permanent means of marking this event will be put in place in the period between now and then. Immediate short-term maintenance projects include conservation work on the roof, gutters, and tower planned for 2008-9. In addition it is proposed that the interior will be repainted, and some conservation work will be carried out to the windows throughout the church. It is also likely that the pews will be replaced by individual chairs as part of this project. Externally the path between the gates and the tower will be renewed and widened while retaining the gravel for the remainder of the grounds. The intention of these works is to continue to secure the fabric of St Andrew's while simultaneously retaining its unique character. These works will allow us to renew St Andrew's one more time and allow this gem of late georgian neo-classical church architecture to continue to serve the spiritual and social needs of the people of Lucan in the twenty-first century as the building heads towards its two hundredth birthday in 2023.

Bibliography

Primary Sources

Leixlip Union Vestry Minute Books RCBL P.0568.

Lucan Vestry Minute Books RCBL P.0913.

Lucan Documents RCBL Box P.0913 & Box 179.

Vestry Minute Book 1822-2008 – Church of Ireland Parish Centre, Lucan.

Mss. Church of Saint Andrew Lucan diocese of Glendalough Record of Gifts and Memorials compiled and presented by Peter T. Hanna 1975 – St Andrew's Church Lucan. Lucan Parish Archive - Church of Ireland Parish Centre Lucan.

Floor plans, Don Cromer Architects.

First report of the commissioners of public instruction, Ireland H.C.1835.

Unpublished Sources

Cromer, Donald, St Andrew's church, Lucan, Co. Dublin, 1823-1993, historical assessment of the church building. Unpublished paper.

Donohoe, Patricia, The Church of Ireland parishes of Leixlip and Lucan in the nineteenth century (M. Litt. thesis, NUI Maynooth 2003).

Donohoe, Patricia, St Andrew's Church Lucan 1823-2003, Pamphlet produced in association with an exhibition to commemorate the one-hundred-and-eightieth anniversary of the construction of St Andrew's.

Secondary Sources

Acheson, Alan, *A history of the Church of Ireland 1691-2001*(Dublin, 2002).

Ball, Francis Elrington, *A history of the county Dublin* (Dublin 1906).

Craig, Maurice, *The architecture of Ireland from the earliest times to 1880* (Dublin, 1987).

Duffy, Hugo, *James Gandon and his times* (Dublin, 1999).

Geissel, Hermann, *A road on the long ridge, in search of the ancient highway on the Esker Riada* (Newbridge, 2006).

Guinness, Desmond, *Lucan House* (Dublin, 2005).

Harbison, Peter, *A thousand years of church heritage in east Galway* (Dublin, 2005).

Hutchison, Sam, *Towers, spires and pinnacles, a history of the cathedrals and churches of the Church of Ireland* (Bray, 2003).

Leslie, Canon J.B. and Wallace, W.J.R. (revised and updated), *Clergy of Dublin and Glendalough, biographical and succession lists* (Belfast, 2001).

McParland, Edward *James Gandon* (London, 1985).

Mulhall, Mary and O'Flynn, Joan, *Treasures of Lucan* (Lucan, 2007).

Mulhall, Mary and O'Flynn, Joan (ed.) *Lucan and Lucanians a revised history of Lucan* (Lucan, 1996).

Pegley, Suzanne (ed.), *Register of the parish of Leixlip, Co. Kildare, 1665-1778* (Dublin, 2001).

Rothery, Sean, *A field guide to the buildings of Ireland* (Dublin, 1997).

Ryan, Christopher (ed.), *Lewis's Dublin, a topographical dictionary of the parishes, towns and villages of Dublin city and county* (Dublin, 2001).

Smyth, William J., 'Exploring the social and cultural topographies of sixteenth and seventeenth century county Dublin' in F.H.A. Aalen and Kevin Whelan (eds.), *Dublin city and county from prehistory to present* (Dublin, 1992).

Smyth, William J., *Map-making, landscapes and memory, a geography of colonial and early modern Ireland c.1530-1750* (Cork, 2006).

Twomey, Valerie, 'St Mary's Church of Ireland parish church, Leixlip, Co. Kildare' in *Aspects of Leixlip* (Leixlip, 2001).

Waddington, Shelagh B., *Welcoming, witnessing and willing to serve, a short history of Lucan Methodist church* (Lucan, ND).

Footnotes

1. For example see the series of twelve volumes of parish registers (i.e. details of christenings, burials and marriages) published by the Parish Register Society of Dublin between 1906 and 1915. The Representative Church Body Library (RCBL), the principal repository in the Church of Ireland's for its archives and manuscripts began a new programme of publications in 1994. To date eleven volumes have been published in the new series including one for the register of St Mary's in Leixlip which includes many references to Lucan parishioners - see Suzanne Pegley (ed.), *Register of the parish of Leixlip, Co. Kildare, 1665-1778* (Dublin, 2001). These registers are invaluable sources for the local historian and they often represent the only permanent record now available of many individuals from previous generations.
2. In the mid-nineteenth century succession lists (i.e. lists of clergy with accompanying brief biographies) were published for a number of Church of Ireland dioceses. At the turn of the twentieth century this work was taken up by Canon James Blenerhasset Leslie who had published eight volumes before his death in 1952. A further nineteen volumes were in typescript. Several of these volumes along with some updated editions of earlier volumes have been printed in the last twenty years. For details of the clergy of Leixlip and Lucan see Canon J.B. Leslie and W.J.R. Wallace (revised and updated), *Clergy of Dublin and Glendalough, biographical and succession lists* (Belfast, 2001), pp 302-5.
3. For a recent work on the important art works often accumulated over many centuries that are visible in even the humblest parish church see Peter Harbison, *A thousand years of church heritage in east Galway* (Dublin, 2005).
4. See Mary Mulhall and Joan O'Flynn, *Treasures of Lucan* (Lucan, 2007) and Mary Mulhall and Joan O'Flynn (ed.) *Lucan and Lucanians a revised history of Lucan* (Lucan, 1996) for brief description of the churches and other landmark buildings of Lucan.
5. In the current organisation of the Church of Ireland Lucan is part of the parish of Leixlip Union in the united diocese of Dublin and Glendalough.
6. Hermann Geissel, *A road on the long ridge, in search of the ancient highway on the Esker Riada* (Newbridge, 2006), pp 10-12.
7. For further details of the ecclesiastical, manorial and succession list history of Lucan and Esker see - William J. Smyth, 'Exploring the social and cultural topographies of sixteenth and seventeenth century county Dublin' in F.H.A. Aalen and Kevin Whelan (eds.), *Dublin city and county from prehistory to present* (Dublin, 1992), pp 121-179, Francis Elrington Ball, *A history of the county Dublin* (Dublin 1906) Vol.iv. pp 35-57 and William J. Smyth, *Map-making, landscapes and memory, a geography of colonial and early modern Ireland* c.1530-1750 (Cork, 2006), pp 225-273 and Canon J.B. Leslie and W.J.R. Wallace (revised and updated), *Clergy of Dublin and Glendalough, biographical and succession lists* (Belfast, 2001), pp 302-5.

8. Alan Acheson, *A history of the Church of Ireland 1691-2001*, (Dublin, 2002), pp 111-2 citing the Beresford Correspondence RCB Vol.VI, No. 238 'Memoirs of the First Fruits Commissioners'.
9. See Sam Hutchison, *Towers, spires and pinnacles, a history of the cathedrals and churches of the Church of Ireland* (Bray, 2003), pp 58-72 for details of the architecture and décor of Board of First Fruits churches.
10. See Valerie Twomey, 'St Mary's Church of Ireland parish church, Leixlip, Co. Kildare' in *Aspects of Leixlip* (Leixlip, 2001) pp. 29-66, for a detailed description of the history , art and architecture of St Mary's parish church in Leixlip. St Mary's is currently undergoing a major conservation programme to secure its future for generations to come.
11. Christopher Ryan (ed.), *Lewis's Dublin, a topographical dictionary of the parishes, towns and villages of Dublin city and county* (Dublin, 2001), pp 204-7.
12. First report of the commissioners of public instruction, Ireland H.C.1835, (45 & 46) and RCBL Lucan Vestry Minute Books P.0913.
13. RCBL Lucan Vestry Minute Books P.0913.
14. Canon J.B. Leslie and W.J.R. Wallace (revised and updated), *Clergy of Dublin and Glendalough, biographical and succession lists* (Belfast, 2001), pp 302-5.
15. Caesar Otway (1780-1842) was born in Nenagh and educated at TCD. He was curate in Leixlip from 1811 to 1822 and the Perpetual Curate of Lucan from 1822 to 1826. He was a prolific author on historical and antiquarian subjects. He published *Sketches of Ireland* (1822) and *A tour in Connaught* (1839). He was co-founder of *The Christian Examiner* in 1825 and *The Dublin Penny Journal* (with the leading artist and antiquarian George Petrie) in 1832.
16. The records for Lucan in the RCBL are P.0913, P.0568 and Lucan Box 179.
17. Vestry Minute book 1822 – 2008 15 July 1824 Lucan Parish Archive.
18. RCBL Lucan Vestry Minute Books P.0913.
19. Memorial in RCBL Box 179 Lucan.
20. Mary Mullhall & Joan O'Flynn, *Treasurers of Lucan* (Lucan, 2007), p. 67.
21. Hugo Duffy, *James Gandon and his times* (Dublin, 1999), p. 265 and Edward McParland, *James Gandon* (London, 1985), p. 106.
22. Desmond Guinness, *Lucan House* (Dublin, 2005), p. 14.
23. RCBL Lucan Vestry Minute Books P.0913.
24. Maurice Craig, *The architecture of Ireland from the earliest times to 1880* (Dublin, 1987) p. 213.
25. Sean Rothery, *A field guide to the buildings of Ireland* (Dublin, 1997), p. 32 and Sam Hutchison, *Towers, spires and pinnacles, a history of the cathedrals and churches of the Church of Ireland* (Bray, 2003), pp 73-82.
26. RCBL Lucan Vestry Minute Books P.0913.
27. RCBL Lucan Vestry Minute Books P.0913.
28. RCBL Lucan Vestry Minute Books P.0913.
29. RCBL Lucan Vestry Minute Books P.0913.The Beresford fund is an investment

fund managed by the RCB the income of which is used to support church building projects.

30. RCBL Lucan Vestry Minute Books P.0913.
31. RCBL Lucan Vestry Minute Books P.0913.
32. RCBL Lucan Vestry Minute Books P.0913.
33. RCBL Lucan Vestry Minute Books P.0913.
34. Mss. Church of Saint Andrew Lucan diocese of Glendalough Record of Gifts and Memorials compiled and presented by Peter T Hanna 1975 – St Andrew's Church Lucan.
35. RCBL Lucan Vestry Minute Books P.0913.
36. RCBL Lucan Vestry Minute Books P.0913.
37. RCBL Lucan Vestry Minute Books P.0913.
38. Peter Harbison, *A thousand years of church heritage in east Galway* (Dublin, 2005), p. xiii.
39. RCBL Lucan Vestry Minute Books P.0913.
40. RCBL Lucan Vestry Minute Books P.0913.
41. RCBL Lucan Vestry Minute Books P.0913.

PROTESTANT PHILANTHROPY *and* SOCIAL INTERACTION IN THE 19TH CENTURY

by Patricia Donohoe

INTRODUCTION

'For what is the Church? The Church is not the clergy: the Church is the clergy and laity.'[1]

The parish in the Church of Ireland, which was the established church until 1869, as well as being a religious entity also constituted a civil unit, acting as a form of minor local government with civil duties and the power to levy taxes for religious and secular purposes. The passing of the Church Temporalities Act in 1833 changed the status of the parish which then no longer had the power to tax the entire population for the religious purposes of the established church.

Lucan parish, as in all Church of Ireland parishes at the time, had certain civil responsibilities towards the poor. These included the appointment of officers of health, the care of deserted children and the provision of coffins for paupers. In tandem with these civil functions, the church also made provision for the poor of the parish, regardless of religious affiliation. Although the civil role lessened over the decades until the church was disestablished,[2] the presence of Church of Ireland residents and those of other reformed churches, which included many of the land, mill and factory owners, influenced the lives of the wider community.

During the nineteenth century the Church of Ireland changed from being a state church of privilege and unequally distributed wealth, to a constitutional church where the laity had a place at every level of church government.[3] The decades between 1800 to 1870 were marked by recurrent crises; popular agitation, tithe wars, famine and the reform of the church all played their part in shaping the life of the parish. After disestablishment, the structure of the parish system changed, the link with the state had been broken and financially the church had to stand alone. Although the involvement of the landed class was always important to the Church of Ireland, following disestablishment this involvement was now more crucial than ever.

Women, who contributed much to church life, were effectively barred from formal participation until 1920. Nevertheless, their contribution, in terms of raising funds for parochial causes and supporting foreign missions, was considerable and their increasing involvement in the parish church can be seen towards the end of the nineteenth century.

Although little exists of a more personal nature in the church records, Lucan parish is fortunate to have in its possession many letters, bills and receipts dating from 1822, some of which give an insight into the hardships experienced by the poor of the parish. Unfortunately because no such records survived for the period of the great famine, its effects on the population of the village can only be noted with reference to census returns and the relief commission papers.

However, the records also show the growing confidence of the Roman Catholic Church. This was reflected by the fact that in 1835 the Roman Catholic priest in Lucan announced that his community no longer wanted Protestant aid. Thereafter, Lucan parish provided help only for Protestant poor, although very occasionally it was noted that a recipient was a member of the Roman Catholic community.

In this essay, we explore the social and philanthropic works of the laity and their involvement in the administration of parochial funds to aid the poor of Lucan.

THE NINETEENTH CENTURY VILLAGE OF LUCAN

In the Irish language the name Lucan or Leamhcan means either the place of the elm tree or a marshy place. Lucan is situated in the barony of Newcastle on the borders of Counties Dublin and Kildare. It was considered to be an area of outstanding beauty, Arthur Young in *A Tour in Ireland* 1776-7 quotes 'the ride from Chapel-Izod [sic]to Lugan [sic] reminds the traveller of the scenery in the vicinity of Heidelburg, in the Palatinate of the Rhine... the swelling land is here clothed in a richly spangled dress of strawberries, peas and flowers, ranging in variegated forms with the winding course of the gentle Liffey.'[4]

The latter part of the eighteenth century had brought prosperity to the village of Lucan, situated on the banks of the River Liffey as it flowed through counties Dublin and Kildare. The presence of mills along the banks of the river provided much needed employment to the inhabitants of the town and the discovery of a spa in Lucan in 1758 attracted the gentry to the area to partake of the waters. As travel became easier during the nineteenth century, people flocked to Lucan which was accessible from Dublin, to visit the spa, and admire the scenery.

The major landowners in Lucan were the Vesey family of Lucan House. Lucan demesne consisted of 137 acres and was valued during the 1840s, for the purpose of Griffith's Valuation, at £367.9s.0d., the largest property in the vicinity.[5] Apart from their main residence the Vesey family also owned fifty-three houses of varying size and value as well as substantial amounts of land.

Amongst the other principal seats in the area were those of James Gandon, son of the architect, who owned twenty-one houses in Lucan as well as some land,[6] Thomas Needham of St Edmondsbury, J. Hamilton Reid of Weston Park, Major-General Sir H. S. Scott of Woodville and Sir John Kingsmill of The Hermitage.[7]

Plate 1: Lucan village from Chapel Hill circa 1900 (looking west). The spire of St Andrew's Church can be seen in the distance

It is impossible to generalise about the importance of the local landlord in Ireland. Miriam Moffitt in her study of the Church of Ireland community of Killala and Achonry, makes the point that the presence of the landlords in the area strengthened the position of the Church of Ireland in the diocese.[8] This can be clearly seen in Lucan where the presence of the major landowner undoubtedly had a positive effect on the village. The involvement of the Vesey family in the local Church of Ireland was considerable. Through the church, generations of the family made a profound contribution to Lucan until the family home was sold in 1925. The Vesey family supported the church and parochial schools generously, and ensured that the poor of the parish were also supported.

A high proportion of the population was employed in agriculture and tourism although the main type of employment for women was in domestic service. However, during the eighteenth century, the milling industry flourished in Lucan and by 1800, Lucan had an iron mill, two corn mills, a paper mill, a linen mill and a saw mill.[9] In 1863, William Strangman Hill, who already owned a woolen mill in Inchicore in Dublin, purchased the iron mill which was situated in Lucan on the banks of the river Liffey, and started a textile factory. Hills Mills remained in family hands and represented the major single source of employment in the Lucan area during the nineteenth century. The mills were famous for their blankets, rug wool, knitting wool, tweeds, worsted and gaberdine, especially in Canada and the United States of America. The mill had its own mill race which in time meant that it could generate much of its own electricity. Hills Woollen Mills closed in 1988 having provided a great source of employment in the Lucan area for 125 years.

Plate 2: Hills Mills, Lucan (looking north), circa 1890 (photograph Jane Wigham Shackleton)

The second great mill in Lucan was the Anna Liffey Mills, also known as Shackleton's Mills. The mill, built in about 1825 as a corn mill, was bought by George Shackleton from Ballytore in County Kildare in 1859, for the purpose of flour milling. The Shackleton family, the oldest established flour millers in Ireland, had been milling products since 1776. Depending upon the time of year, the mill operated up to three eight-hour shifts per day and in the early 1900s employed between fifty and sixty people. The location of the mills was all important, firstly they were near Dublin and secondly they were on the banks of the river, which provided them with their motive power, firstly with water power, and then in 1905, when the water wheels were replaced by water turbines, producing electricity.

As with Hills Mills, Shackletons Mills gave employment to generations of Lucan people.

Plate 3: Shackletons Mills circa 1900 (photograph by Jane Wigham Shackleton)

SOCIAL CONDITIONS IN LUCAN

Samuel Lewis in the *Topographical Directory of Ireland* described Lucan as a 'post town and parish ....seven miles from Dublin, on the mail road to Galway and Sligo.'[10] The town 'beautifully situated in a fertile vale on the eastern bank of the River Liffey... the soil fertile and the crops abundant... with well built houses which were used as lodging-houses during the summer season.'[11] However, there certainly was hardship in Lucan during the 1820s and 1830s, and many of the inhabitants suffered from poverty, illness and disease. Diseases which are not life-threatening today, often claimed lives during the nineteenth century. In 1868 whooping cough and scarletina were rife in the village and caused the death of several children. The local doctor, Thomas Purefoy, who was a member of the established church, serving both on the vestry and as churchwarden, cared for those suffering from the diseases, including one of his own children, until scarletina finally claimed his own life on 23 December 1868.[12] A three-panel stained glass window was erected in St Andrew's Church in his memory by his wife and children.

Unfortunately, as mentioned earlier, there are no surviving poor accounts for the Church of Ireland parish of Lucan for the period encompassing the years of the great famine. However, police inspectors and officers were required, from 1845, to report to Dublin Castle as to the state of the potato crop in Dublin county. Although much of the agricultural land of Lucan adjoined that of Leixlip, in County Kildare where the potato blight decimated the crop in 1846, in Lucan, both the early and late crops of potato suffered only a 10% loss through the effects of blight.[13]

The census returns for the Lucan area in the years 1841, 1851 and 1861 have been studied to ascertain whether the population of Lucan declined during the famine years. In 1841, the population of Lucan was almost equally divided between the town and the rural areas, with 563 inhabitants in the town and 576 living in the rural area. The numbers in the town changed marginally in the census of 1851, falling to 535, while the number living in rural Lucan decreased from 576 to 474. However, the most dramatic change took

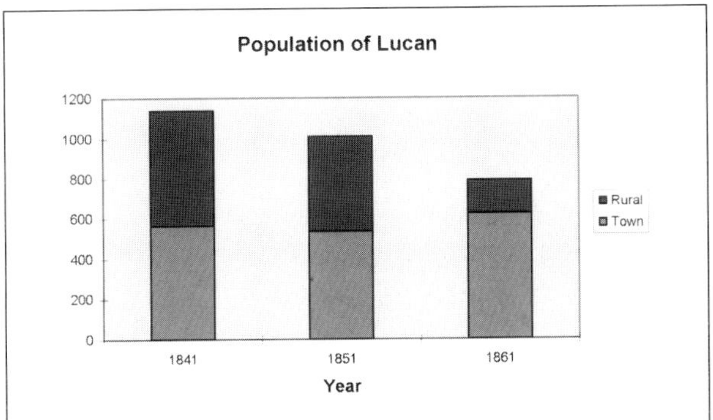

Table 1.1: Source: Census of Ireland for the years 1841, 1851 and 1861

place in the period between 1851 and 1861, when the population of the town increased to 634 while that of the rural area plummeted to a mere 167 persons (see table 1.1). These statistics indicate that while the famine affected Lucan to some extent, especially in the rural area, the population in the town began to recover quite rapidly. This may have been helped by the opening of the Shackleton Mills in 1859 which brought increased employment into the town.

In the census of 1841, 17% of the housing available in Lucan was classified as fourth class (see table 1.2). This class comprised of a one roomed thatched mud cabin without windows. However, by 1851, this type of housing had almost disappeared, declining to 4%. Two other classes of housing had increased during the decade, the biggest increase, being in second class housing which had increased by 10% (see table 1.3). The number of third class housing decreased only marginally.

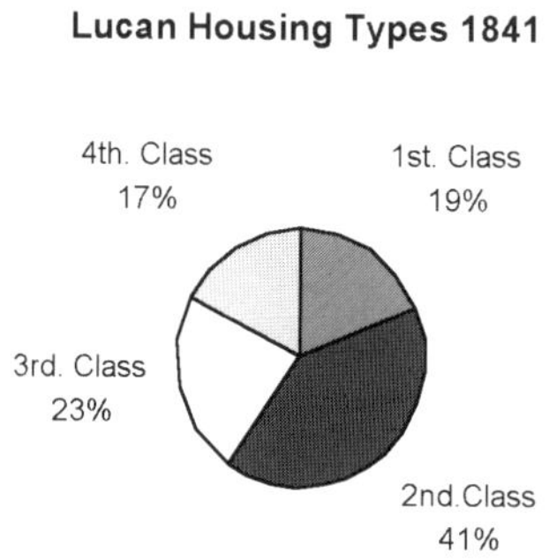

Table 1.2 (Source: Census of Ireland 1841)

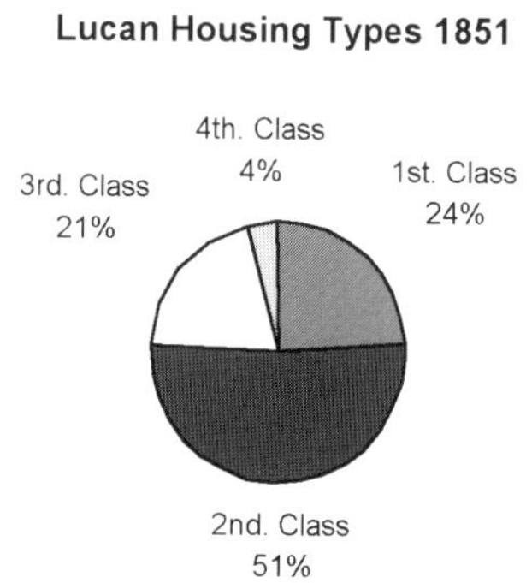

Table 1.3 (Source: Census of Ireland 1851)

It is interesting to compare the statistics for the different class of houses before and after the famine in Lucan. The number of 4th class housing fell from 17% in 1841 to 4% in 1851. While there was an increase in 1st and 2nd class housing, 3rd class showed a slight decrease. Overall, it appears that in the decades after the famine, Lucan benefited by new industry coming into the area, which brought with it the owners and managers of the new mills who built houses and settled in the vicinity.

The picture of Lucan therefore which emerges after the famine is one of employment and prosperity. The presence in the town of the Vesey family, as well as many of the gentry, mill and factory owners, who, although not all members of the established church, were mostly Protestant, ensured that the profile of the Protestant churches, which began with the building of St Andrew's Church in 1823, remained high during the remainder of the century.

THE CIVIL DUTIES OF THE PARISH

August 1833 saw a major upheaval in the Church of Ireland with the passing of the Church Temporalities Act. This act, which was amended in 1834, changed the structure of the established church and the status of the parish, which now no longer had the power to tax the entire population for the religious purposes of the established church. This tax had been used to pay for the physical maintenance of the church and the repayment of the loan from the Board of First Fruits, the purchase of sacramental bread and wine, coal, turf and candles for the church, the washing of the church linens, the cleaning of the church, and for the payment of minor church officers. Parishes therefore became purely religious bodies, the right to levy a tax for secular purposes, such as providing for abandoned children as well as the provision of parish coffins, having been abolished in the previous decade.[14] However, John Crawford makes the point that in areas where Protestant influence still pertained, the vestry's responsibility for the collection of parish and grand jury cess continued until 1870.[15] It appears that this may have been the case in Lucan where for some years following the passing of the act, sums of money were still being levied to provide for maintenance for deserted children and coffins for the poor.

The parish cess accounts for 1825 record that a sum of £86.1s.0d. was applotted for that year.[16] This figure included the arrears from the previous year, which amounted to £6.5s.5d. These taxes were to be raised and levied 'by distress or otherwise' from the parish of Lucan and Esker. Understandably the imposition of a tax on those who were not members of the established church led in some instances to protests, or near riotous behaviour, at some Easter vestries throughout the country.[17] Although there is no mention of such behaviour at Easter vestries in Lucan parish, in 1827 a dispute arose as to the legality of the method used for applotting the parish cess. The main difficulty seems to have been the custom, which had prevailed in the Union of Leixlip (which included Lucan and Esker), of assessing all the land in the parish, regardless of the quality, on the same basis.

In 1830 the parish sought the legal advice of Sergeant [sic] J. Blackburne who found that 'the custom that an inhabitant should be assessed according to the quantity and not the quantity and quality of his land [was] plainly repugnant and that the method used was not legal.'[18] The matter may not have been resolved, as it is noted in the vestry minutes that 'the collectors of the parish cess be allowed at the rate of 1s. in the pound for the collection of the cess for the current year, in consideration of the extraordinary trouble and fatigue incurred by them in making the last collection.'[19] The following year the applotters of the parish cess were paid an extra £5 'in compensation for their trouble and loss of time.'[20] However, with the passing of the Church Temporalities Act in 1833, the system used for the raising

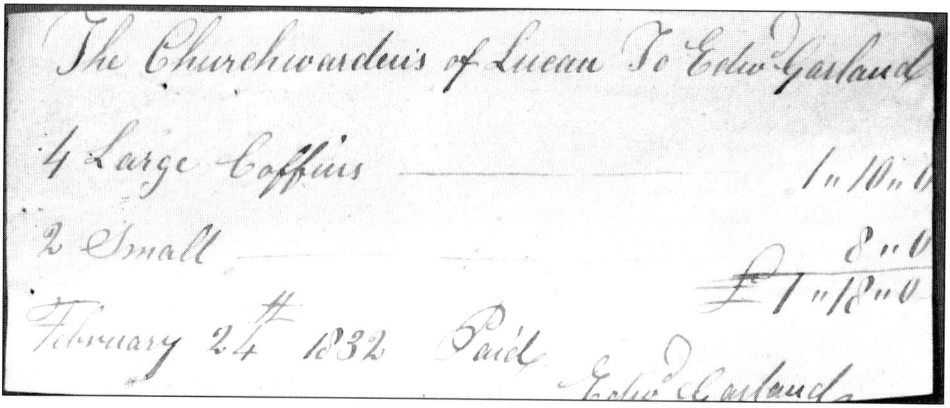
The Churchwardens of Lucan To Edwd Garland

4 Large Coffins 1 " 10 " 0

2 Small 8 " 0

£1 " 18 " 0

February 24th 1832 Paid

Edwd Garland

Plate 4: Bill for making of parish coffins - folder dated 1832, RCBL P.09123.27

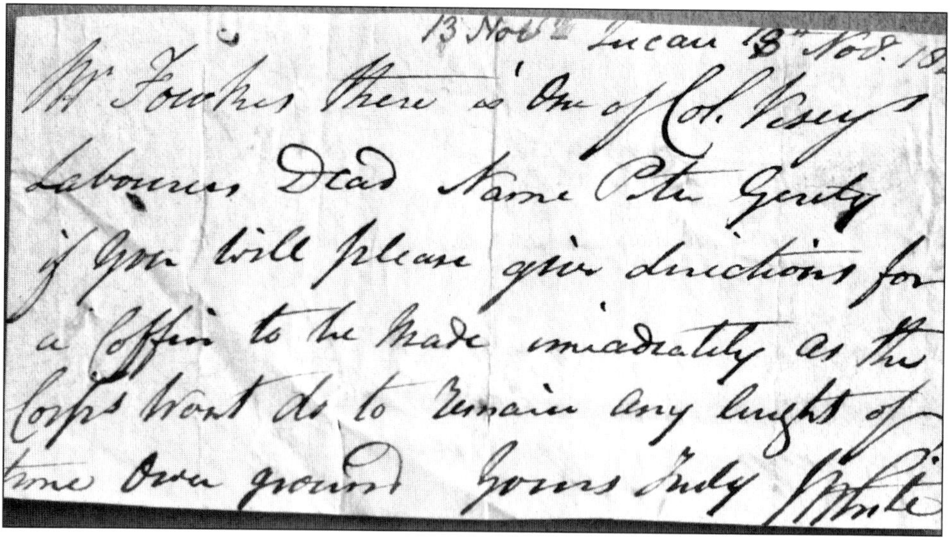
13 Nov Lucan 13th Novr 18

Mr Fowkes there is One of Col. Vesey's Labourers Dead Name Peter Gerity if You will please give directions for a Coffin to be Made imediately as the Corps wont do to remain any lenghts of time over ground Yours Truly J White

Plate 5: Request for parish coffin - folder dated 1825, RCBL P.0913.27

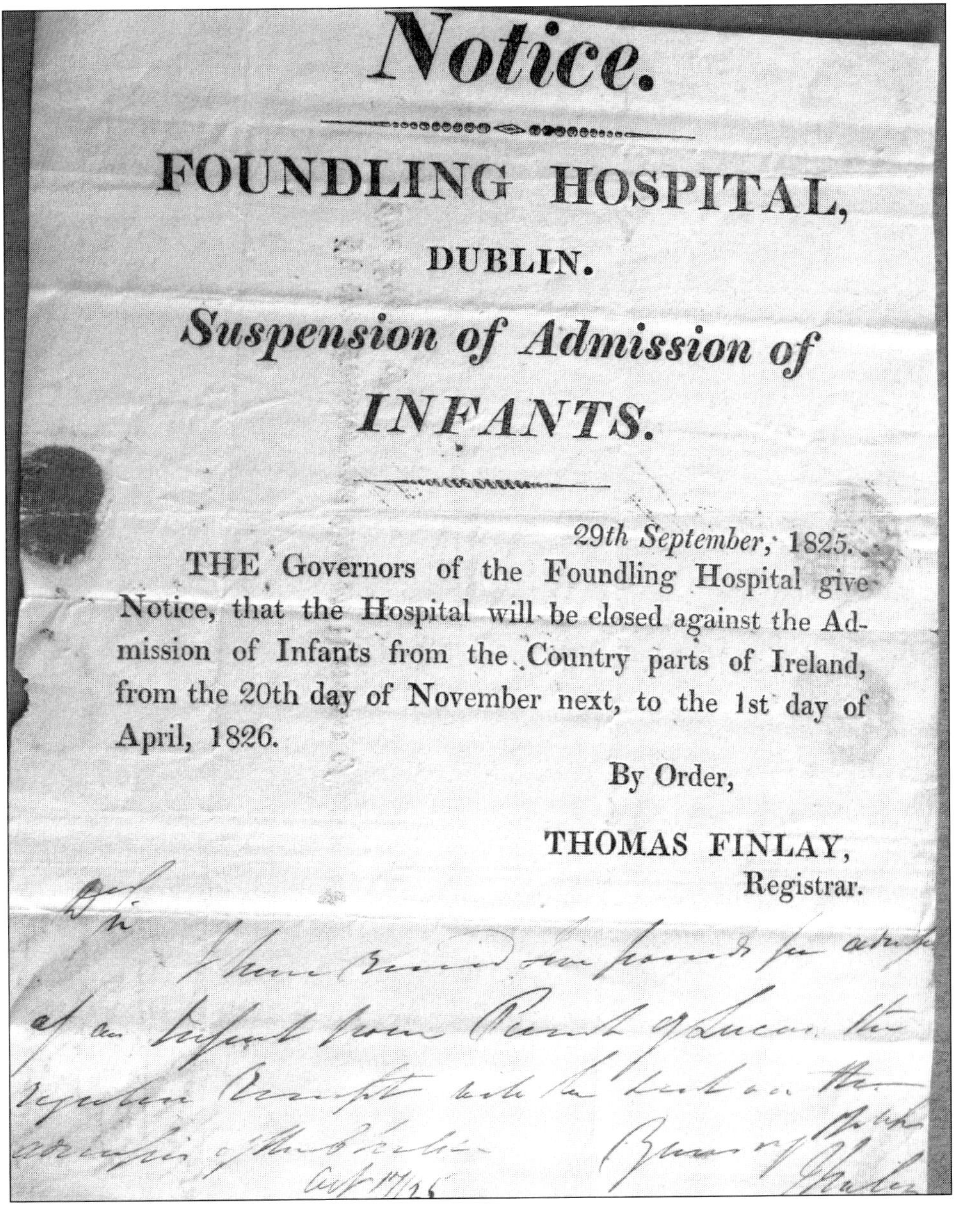

Notice.

FOUNDLING HOSPITAL,

DUBLIN.

Suspension of Admission of

INFANTS.

29th September, 1825.

THE Governors of the Foundling Hospital give Notice, that the Hospital will be closed against the Admission of Infants from the Country parts of Ireland, from the 20th day of November next, to the 1st day of April, 1826.

By Order,

THOMAS FINLAY,
Registrar.

Plate 6: Notice in folder dated 1825, RCBL P0913.27

of parish cess, that is, the setting of the tax at the annual Easter vestry, had disappeared in most parts of the country.[21] As a result, Irish parishes became solely religious bodies. This was also the case in Lucan parish, where 1833 was the last year in which parish cess was raised in that manner.

As a civil parish one of the duties of the Church of Ireland was the provision of coffins for paupers. Occasionally the cause of death was recorded, for example, in 1824 coffins were required for a women who had died of breast cancer and one who had died of a fever. Although no trend can be discerned as to the main cause of death during the 1820s, what can be clearly seen is the abject poverty in which some members of the community were living, that they had to appeal for a coffin in which to bury their relative. A local man, Owen Coogan, made the coffins for the parish, the usual price being 10s. for an adult coffin with a lesser amount for the coffin of a child. In addition to this was the cost of digging a grave, which in the 1820s was 1s.6d.

In some cases concern was expressed to have the dead interred speedily. In September 1825, when a ploughman, 'Old Robinson' died, a large coffin was ordered for him (costing 13s.) to be sent 'early in the morning to have him removed from the hospital and interred, as it was deemed imprudent to have him waked.'[22] Two months later a coffin was ordered to be made immediately for one of Colonel Vesey's labourers, 'as the corpse won't do to remain any length of time over ground.'[23] The reasons for this haste was not given, but possibly the men had died of a contagious disease and it was feared that the bodies might cause infection.

Provision was also made for the care of abandoned children. It was common practice in some areas for such children to be cared for in the parish, although there appears to have been no suitable accommodation for such cases in Lucan. In October 1825 the parish of Lucan paid £5 to the Foundling Hospital in Dublin to enable a child to be admitted there. The Foundling Hospital, which was situated in St James's Street, was originally built as a workhouse in 1703 but was converted to cater for foundlings in 1730, after it was discovered that half the inmates who had been taken off the streets were children. The hospital must have been under severe strain during 1825 as a notice was send out to parishes in September of that year announcing that 'the hospital would be closed against the admission of infants from the country parts of Ireland from 20 November to 1 April 1826'.[24] In 1839 the building reverted once again to become a workhouse, this time for the South Dublin Union.[25]

CARING FOR THE POOR OF THE PARISH

A collection was taken up during the Sunday morning and evening services and an offertory made during the monthly celebration of Holy Communion. This money was disposed of to such 'pious and charitable uses as the minister and churchwardens shall think fit'.[26] In Lucan parish this money was put into a fund which was used to support those in need. The amount given by those receiving Holy Communion, on average, far exceeded the amount taken up at the normal Sunday collection, perhaps reflecting the fact that during the early and middle nineteenth century those who received the sacrament were generally the elite of the parish.

Lucan parish is fortunate that it has in its possession a quantity of invoices, receipts and letters for the period 1822-32.[27] The correspondence gives an indication of the type of aid that was requested for, and provided to, the poor in Lucan during that time. At the beginning of the 1820s requests for aid were made on behalf of the poor by either the incumbent or the parish clerk to the churchwardens of the parish. Towards the end of the 1820s, men who indicated that they paid parish cess also signed many requests. Although poor account books prior to 1850 have not survived in Lucan parish, receipts for the period 1822-32 indicate that large quantities of coal, turf, oat and wheat meal were purchased on a weekly basis for distribution to the poor of the parish.

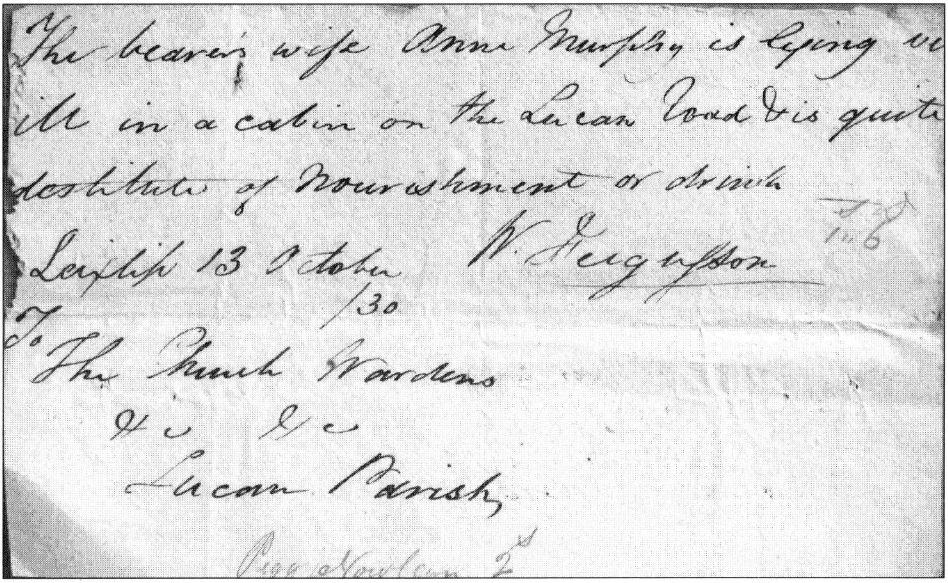
The bearer's wife Anne Murphy is lying ve
ill in a cabin on the Lucan Road & is quite
destitute of Nourishment or drink
Leixlip 13 October W. Fergusson
/30
To The Church Wardens
&c &c
Lucan Parish

Plate 7: Application to Lucan Parish for help for an ill woman. Folder dated 1830, RCBL P.0913.27

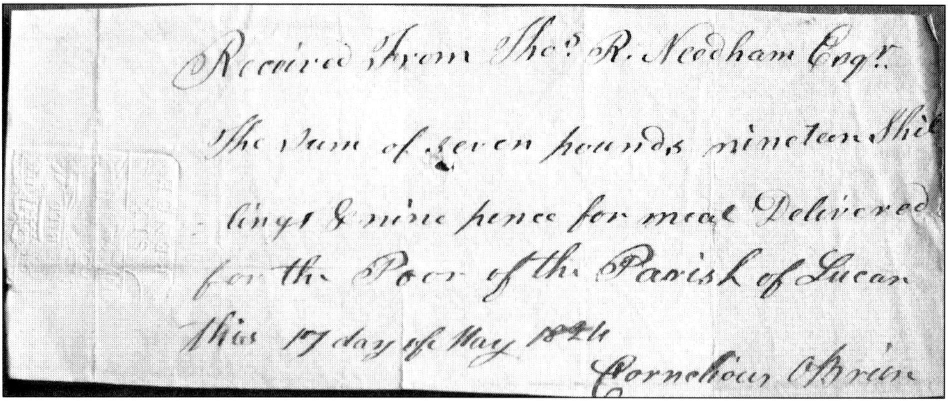

Received from Thos R. Needham Esqr.
The sum of seven pounds nineteen Shil
lings & nine pence for meal Delivered
for the Poor of the Parish of Lucan
this 17 day of May 1824
Cornelius O'Brien

Plate 8: Order for purchase of meal for poor of Lucan. Folder dated 1824, RCBL P.0913.27

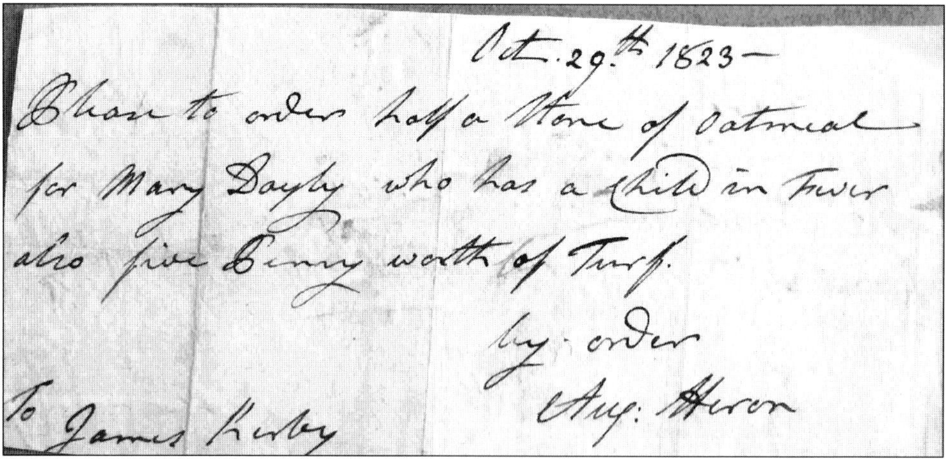

Oct. 29th 1823—
Please to order half a Stone of Oatmeal
for Mary Dayly who has a Child in Fever
also five Penny worth of Turf.
by order
Aug: Heron
To James Kirby

Plate 9: Order for purchase of meal and turf for poor of Lucan. Folder dated 1823, RCBL P.0913.27

Clothing was also provided on a regular basis. In 1824 complete outfits were ordered for 'three poor women belonging to the Church of Lucan.'[28] The women, Mrs Sheeran, Mrs Pointon and Mrs Reed were all widows.[29] These outfits were ordered by Emily Vesey (wife of the then church warden) and comprised calico gowns, check aprons, linen shifts, petticoats, stockings, flannel waistcoats and muslin caps. Three shawls were also ordered at a cost of 2s.6d. each. The cost of material and making all of the above amounted to £3.15s.7d. Shoes were then provided at a cost of 19s.6d. for three pairs.[30] The means to pay for these outfits was provided from the

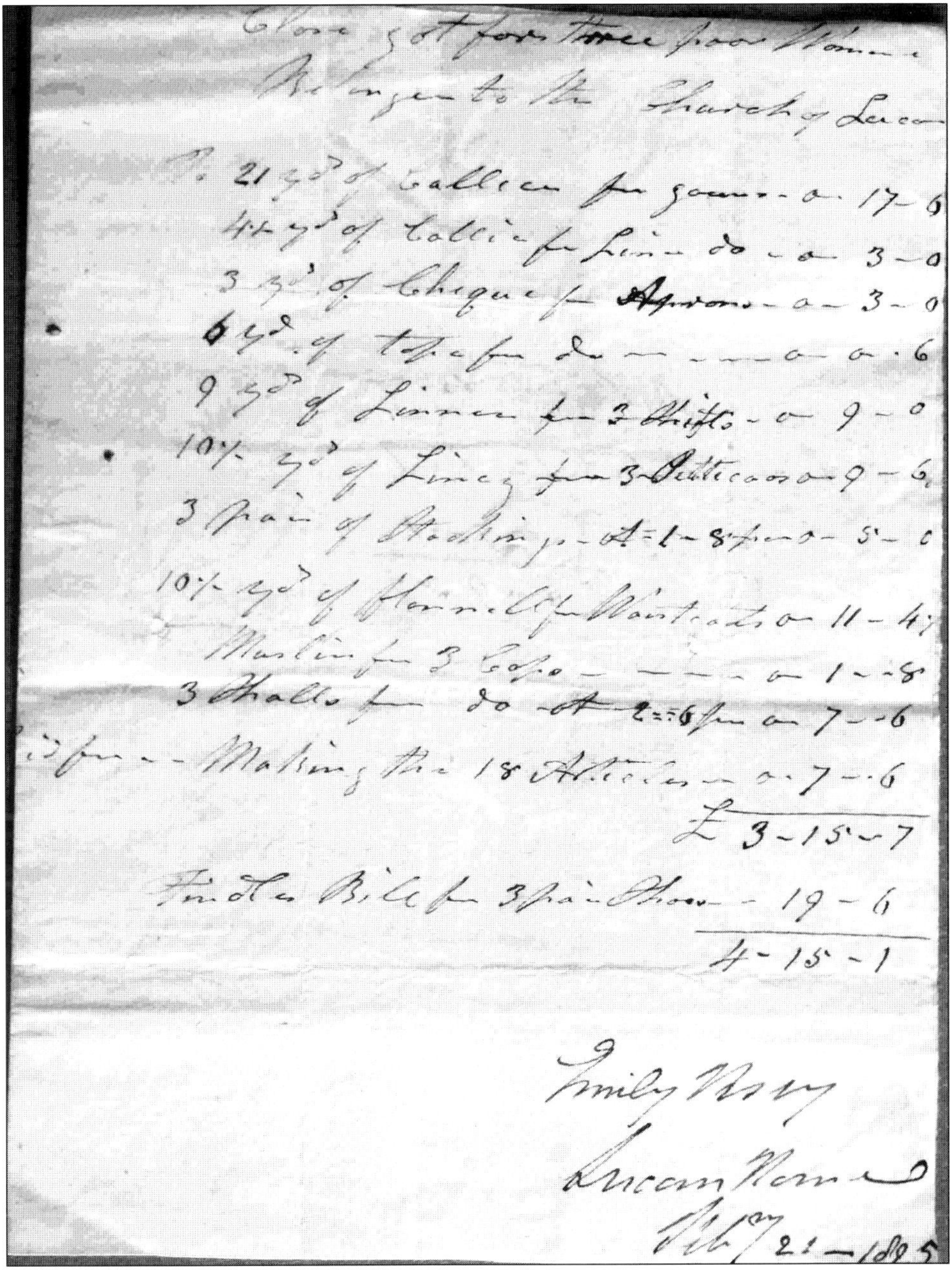

Cloaths got for three poor Women
Belonging to the Church of Lucan

21 yds of Callico for gowns – 0 – 17 – 6
4½ yds of Callico for Lining do – 0 – 3 – 0
3 yds of Cheque for Aprons – 0 – 3 – 0
6 yds of Tape for do – – – 0 – 0 – 6
9 yds of Linnen for 3 Shifts – 0 – 9 – 0
10½ yds of Linsey for 3 Petticoats 0 – 9 – 6
3 pair of Stockings at 1 – 8 pair 0 – 5 – 0
10½ yds of Flannell for Waistcoats 0 – 11 – 4½
Muslin for 3 Caps – – – 0 – 1 – 8
3 Shawls for do at 2 – 6 per 0 – 7 – 6
Paid for Making the 18 Articles 0 – 7 – 6
£ 3 – 15 – 7
Findlas Bill for 3 pair Shoes – 19 – 6
4 – 15 – 1

Emily Vesey
Lucan House
Feby 21 – 1825

Plate 10: Order for clothing for widows of Lucan parish. Folder dated 1825, RCBL P.0913.27

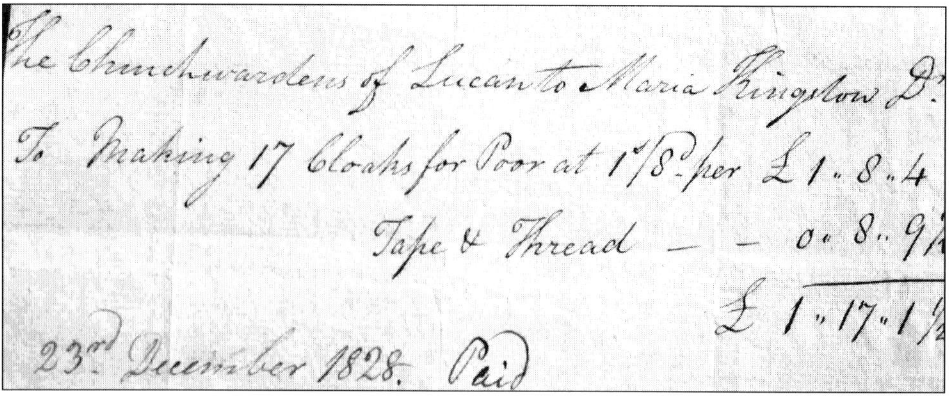
The Churchwardens of Lucan to Maria Kingston Dr
To Making 17 Cloaks for Poor at 1/8 per £1.8.4
Tape & Thread — — 0.8.9½
£1.17.1½
23rd December 1828. Paid

Plate 11: Bill for making cloaks for poor of Lucan. Folder dated 1828, RCBL P.0913.27

poor fund. This was not an isolated expenditure, the following year saw yet another three women provided for out of the poor fund, again at the request of Emily Vesey.

However, normally clothing was provided at the request of the churchwardens, rector or parish clerk. In 1828 Maria Kingston was paid £1.17s.1½d. for making seventeen cloaks for the poor, included in this was the cost of tape and thread. Men were also provided with clothing, 4s.6d. was the cost of one large suit and 3s. for one small suit in 1828.[31]

During the first week of January 1831 a total of eighteen blankets, fifteen cloaks and six great coats were distributed to those on the poor list.[32] Other essentials, which continued to be provided throughout the year, included gowns, shifts, petticoats, waistcoats, shirts, caps, aprons and shoes. Many of these garments continued to be made by Maria Kingston. Maria's name appears again in 1830, as the sextoness of the church for which she was paid £12 per annum. She also washed the church linen, being paid £1 per annum for the work, but it appears that her main employment was as a seamstress. Other members of the Kingston family were also involved within the parish, John Kingston was the bell ringer and William Kingston appears to have been both schoolmaster and parish clerk for some time.

Although the Church of Ireland parish administered the poor fund, religion was not a barrier to receiving aid, although occasionally it was mentioned in the request. In 1828 the Reverend Fielding Ould (perpetual curate of Lucan Parish 1827-36), writing on behalf of one Sally McNamara, describes her as an 'extremely poor and very deserving creature who has been fourteen years living in this parish and had never received any parochial assistance whatever.'[33] Reverend Ould requested that she be given half a crown for the present and if possible that she be put on the church poor list, adding that she is a Roman Catholic.

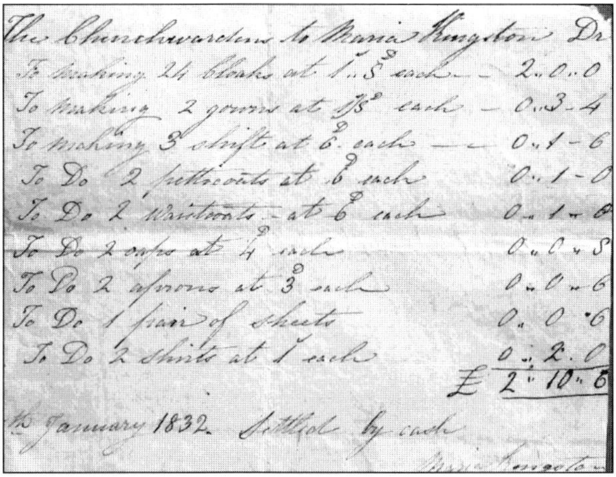

The Churchwardens to Maria Kingston Dr

To making 24 cloaks at 1..8d each	—	2..0..0
To making 2 gowns at 1/8d each	—	0..3..4
To making 3 shift at 6d each	—	0..1..6
To Do 2 petticoats at 6d each		0..1..0
To Do 2 waistcoats at 6d each		0..1..0
To Do 2 caps at 4d each		0..0..8
To Do 2 aprons at 3d each		0..0..6
To Do 1 pair of sheets		0..0..6
To Do 2 shirts at 1s each		0..2..0
	£	2..10..6

[illegible] January 1832 Settled by cash

Maria Kingston

Plate 12: Bill from Maria Kingston for making clothes for poor of Lucan. Folder dated 1832 in RCBL, P.0913.27

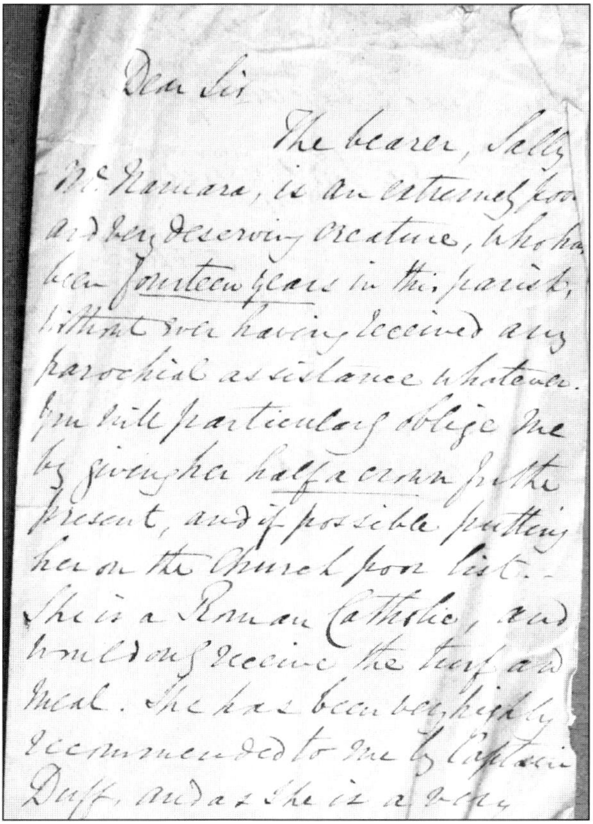

Dear Sir

The bearer, Sally McNamara, is an extremely poor and very deserving creature, who has been fourteen years in this parish, without ever having received any parochial assistance whatever. You will particularly oblige me by giving her half a crown for the present, and if possible putting her on the Church poor list. — She is a Roman Catholic, and would only receive the turf and meal. She has been very highly recommended to me by Captain Duff, and as she is a very

Plate 13: Request for aid for Roman Catholic in Lucan. n/d in folders RCBL P.0913.27

However this situation changed in 1835. A vestry meeting held on 25 May had to be adjourned because of the 'violent proceedings of the Roman Catholic inhabitants of the parish, stimulated and encouraged by their priest...where it was repeatedly stated that Protestant assistance was not needed for the support of Roman Catholic poor, Roman Catholics were able and willing to support their own poor.'[34] Following the abandoned meeting, Protestant inhabitants of the parish were invited to a meeting in the vestry room, chaired by James Gandon, to 'consider the propriety of making a change in the ordinary distribution of the weekly collections.'[35] A resolution moved by Major John Wills and seconded by William Gorman, stated that:

> it appears that whereas the Roman Catholic paupers of this parish have been receiving nearly to the amount of £100 annually out of our Sunday and other collections, in weekly sums of money and annual supplies of blankets and cloaks, and this for several years past, while not more than six or seven Protestant names appear on the poor lists; and whereas it has been signified to us by the leading Roman Catholic authorities that it is their desire and intention henceforward to support their own poor, independently of, without the necessity of having recourse to Protestant means of contributions; it is the unanimously opinion of us whose names are hereunto subscribed, that all Roman Catholic paupers on our poor list be immediately transferred to their fellow worshippers for that support which they have hitherto most cheerfully received from us.[36]

This incident possibly reflects the greater confidence and assertiveness of the Roman Catholic church following the removal of the remaining penal laws.

An examination of the poor account book for the period 1850-65 indicates that the Protestant poor of the parish were still in receipt of aid.[37] The accounts show that from 1850 to 1855 every penny received was spent, all on the poor and the sick, this perhaps is an indication that the effects of the famine were still being felt in the Lucan area. Extra relief was also provided during times of extreme hardship, as in February 1853 when there were such heavy falls of snow that the evening service had to be cancelled. In addition to cash payments, clothes, shoes, coal, turf and Christmas dinners were provided for those in need.

The parish poor lists are more than impersonal lines in a book, often recording the name and circumstances of the recipient. The same names occur frequently, with most receiving aid mainly in the form of cash, but also coal and turf, on a weekly basis. Special mention was made of the provision of clothes and shoes from the poor fund which enabled children to attend school. However, not all of the money taken up during service was always used to give aid to the poor. The vestry had the power to vote sums of money from the collection for special purposes and causes. These included the purchase of bibles, prayer and hymnbooks for the parish and hymnbooks and 'rewards' for the children who attended Sunday school. The parochial lending library was also in receipt of money granted by the vestry. In 1856 there was a surplus of income over expenditure, this surplus was carried forward to the following years, thus providing a buffer against future expenditure. The amounts expended were not large: in the year from April 1860 to March 1861 the total collection and offertory amounted to £38.2s.6d., most of which was went to alleviate the distress of the poor.[38]

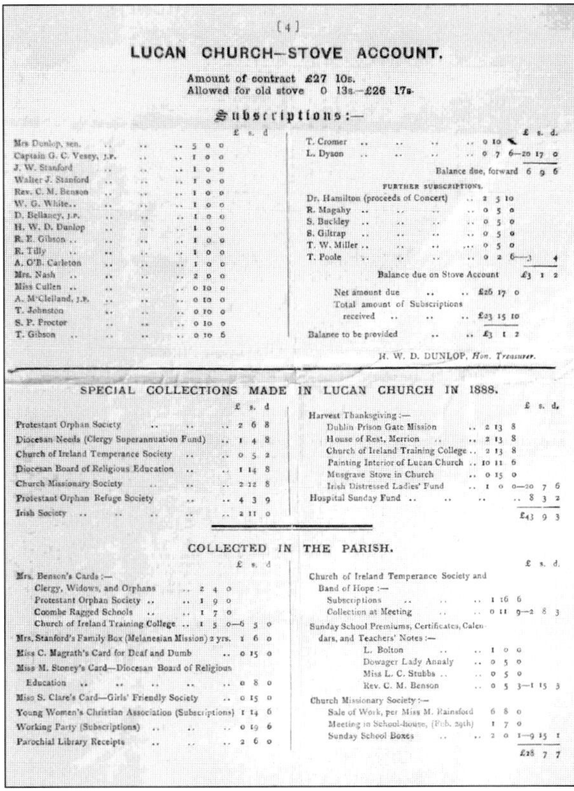

[4]

LUCAN CHURCH—STOVE ACCOUNT.

Amount of contract £27 10s.
Allowed for old stove 0 13s.—£26 17s.

Subscriptions:—

	£	s.	d
Mrs Dunlop, sen.	5	0	0
Captain G. C. Vesey, J.P.	1	0	0
J. W. Stanford	1	0	0
Walter J. Stanford	1	0	0
Rev. C. M. Benson	1	0	0
W. G. White	1	0	0
D. Bellaney, J.P.	1	0	0
H. W. D. Dunlop	1	0	0
R. E. Gibson	1	0	0
R. Tilly	1	0	0
A. O'B. Carleton	1	0	0
Mrs. Nash	2	0	0
Miss Cullen	0	10	0
A. M'Clelland, J.P.	0	10	0
T. Johnston	0	10	0
S. P. Proctor	0	10	0
T. Gibson	0	10	6

	£ s. d.	£ s. d.
T. Cromer	0 10 0	
L. Dyson	0 7 6	20 17 0
Balance due, forward		6 9 6
FURTHER SUBSCRIPTIONS.		
Dr. Hamilton (proceeds of Concert)	2 5 10	
R. Magahy	0 5 0	
S. Buckley	0 5 0	
S. Giltrap	0 5 0	
T. W. Miller	0 5 0	
T. Poole	0 2 6	3 4
Balance due on Stove Account		£3 1 2

	£ s. d.
Net amount due	£26 17 0
Total amount of Subscriptions received	£23 15 10
Balance to be provided	£3 1 2

H. W. D. DUNLOP, *Hon. Treasurer.*

SPECIAL COLLECTIONS MADE IN LUCAN CHURCH IN 1888.

	£	s.	d
Protestant Orphan Society	2	6	8
Diocesan Needs (Clergy Superannuation Fund)	1	4	8
Church of Ireland Temperance Society	0	5	2
Diocesan Board of Religious Education	1	14	8
Church Missionary Society	2	12	8
Protestant Orphan Refuge Society	4	3	9
Irish Society	2	11	0

	£ s. d.	£ s. d.
Harvest Thanksgiving:—		
Dublin Prison Gate Mission	2 13 8	
House of Rest, Merrion	2 13 8	
Church of Ireland Training College	2 13 8	
Painting Interior of Lucan Church	10 11 6	
Musgrave Stove in Church	0 15 0	
Irish Distressed Ladies' Fund	1 0 0	20 7 6
Hospital Sunday Fund		8 3 2
		£43 9 3

COLLECTED IN THE PARISH.

	£ s. d	£ s. d
Mrs. Benson's Cards:—		
Clergy, Widows, and Orphans	2 4 0	
Protestant Orphan Society	1 9 0	
Coombe Ragged Schools	1 7 0	
Church of Ireland Training College	1 5 0	6 5 0
Mrs. Stanford's Family Box (Melanesian Mission) 2 yrs.		1 6 0
Miss C. Magrath's Card for Deaf and Dumb		0 15 0
Miss M. Stoney's Card—Diocesan Board of Religious Education		0 8 0
Miss S. Clare's Card—Girls' Friendly Society		0 15 0
Young Women's Christian Association (Subscriptions)		1 14 6
Working Party (Subscriptions)		0 19 6
Parochial Library Receipts		2 6 0

	£ s. d.	£ s. d.
Church of Ireland Temperance Society and Band of Hope:—		
Subscriptions	1 16 6	
Collection at Meeting	0 11 9	2 8 3
Sunday School Premiums, Certificates, Calendars, and Teachers' Notes:—		
L. Bolton	1 0 0	
Dowager Lady Annaly	0 5 0	
Miss L. C. Stubbs	0 5 0	
Rev. C. M. Benson	0 5 3	1 15 3
Church Missionary Society:—		
Sale of Work, per Miss M. Rainsford	6 8 0	
Meeting in School-house, (Feb. 29th)	1 7 0	
Sunday School Boxes	2 0 1	9 15 1
		£28 7 7

Plate 14: Parish accounts showing monies raised for different charitable purposes. 1888. RCBL P.0913.27

Church collections were also held on a regular basis for a wide variety of special causes. During the same period these amounted to £31.1s.11d. Among the recipients were the Irish Society, the Jews Society, the Church Mission Society, the Clergy Widows, and the parochial schools. Other societies which benefited during the nineteenth century were the Church Education Society, the Irish Church Missions, widows and families of soldiers, orphan refugees and the Protestant Orphan Society. A guest preacher was often invited to take part in these services, which usually had a larger congregation than was normally the case. Apart from these regular appeals, there were, on occasions, special appeals. In 1861 an appeal for the Indian famine relief fund realised the sum of £8.16s.11d. and the following year a collection held for the Lancashire distress fund raised £10.19s.0d.[39]

Plate 15: St Andrew's parochial school, Main St, Lucan, (Courtesy of the late Bertie White)

THE PAROCHIAL SCHOOLS

On 27 February 1827, Lucan vestry met to approve a site for the erection of a parochial school to cater for the parish children in Lucan.[40] For the previous eighteen months William Kingston had been acting schoolmaster. He had received no remuneration, there being no fund available from which to pay him. The vestry resolved to pay Kingston £5 out of the poor fund for his work.[41] The children, twelve boys and eighteen girls, who each paid 1d. per week for their education, were taught in the vestry room of St Andrew's Church.[42] The new school was built opposite the church on a site which had formerly been part of the road to the old bridge over the river. It was decided that a loan would be obtained to build the school from £55.7s.8d. bank stock which remained out of funds raised for building the church. This was to be repaid by installments, the money coming mainly from the collection taken at an annual service which was to be held in Lucan church for the benefit of the school.[43]

In 1836 a second school was built on the same site to cater for infants. This cost £60, although extra work, which included the building of walls, cost a further £25.2s.[44] This was paid for from a legacy of £50 left to the school by the late Colonel George Vesey and two special collections in Lucan church, which between them realised more than £52.[45] The schoolhouses remained in use until 1972 when the new St Andrew's school was built, and thereafter the infant school served as a parish hall until it was demolished in 1996.

The schools catered for both boys and girls and experienced some difficulty in the early years in providing the essentials necessary to enable some of the children of the parish to attend. In 1829 the curate, Reverend Ould, acknowledged the receipt of two guineas from an unnamed benefactor, to pay for twelve pairs of shoes for the children of the parish school. However, he was also looking for some coal, for which he wrote 'we are in great distress.'[46] Subsequently the cost of fuel for heating the schools was paid for out of money accruing from the rent of pews in the church.[47]

The Second Report of the Commissioners of Irish Education enquiry reveals that there were also a number of other schools in the Lucan area; all except one charged fees. The largest of these was a school where one hundred Roman Catholic children were educated by James and Anne Lynch. Although fee-paying, the school was also supported from the proceeds of an annual charity sermon preached in the Roman Catholic Church. The schoolhouse was built by public subscription. James McWilliams educated twenty-two boys, eighteen of whom were members of the established church, in his own home and a school was held in the home of Colonel Hanfield of the Hermitage, Lucan, where twenty 'poor Roman Catholics were taught by the ladies of Colonel Hanfield's family.' There was a pay school where thirty Roman Catholic children were taught by Charles Duffy, and an evening school was held in Esker where twelve children were educated.[48]

As noted above, the parochial schools were in receipt of the proceeds from an annual charity service in the church. In 1851 this amounted to £13.0s.5d. In addition to this, donations to the school realised a further £16.11s.6d.[49] The list of contributors to the school funds makes interesting reading, and includes donations from Arthur Lee Guinness and the Rt Hon. Benjamin Lee Guinness, grandsons of Arthur Guinness, the founder of Guinness's brewery.[50] The Guinness family had a long association with the parishes of Leixlip Union.[51] It was in Leixlip that Arthur and his father Richard established their first brewery, a forerunner to the brewery subsequently established by Arthur at St James's Gate in Dublin. The Vesey family were also generous benefactors to the school, Mrs Emily Vesey not only contributed directly to the fund but also gave £10 a year towards the salary of the school-mistress.[52] Her daughter, Lady Elizabeth Colthurst, paid for the provision of bread for the children attending the infant school.[53] When Elizabeth died in 1839, her mother, who lived until 1853, continued her daughter's payments for bread for the infants.[54]

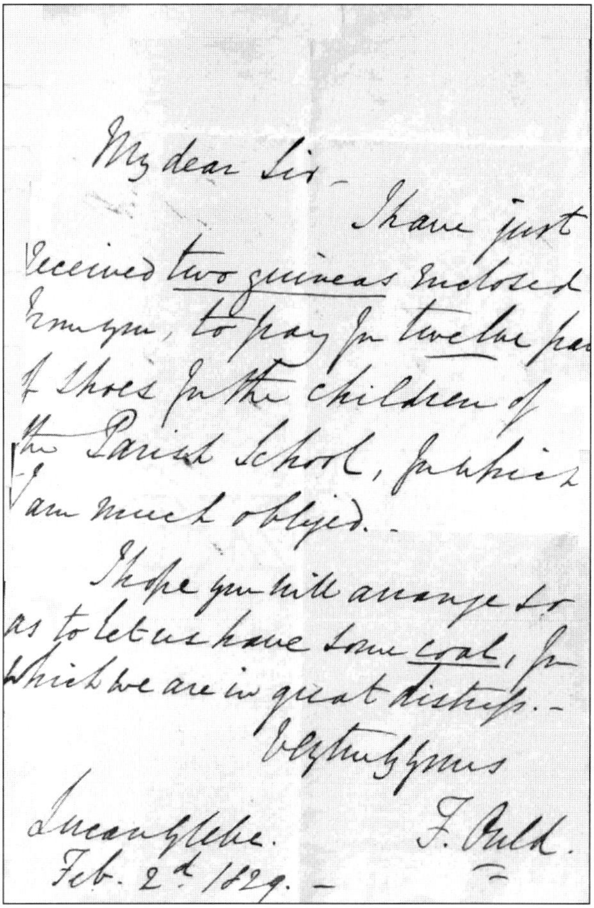
My dear Sir —
I have just received two guineas enclosed from you, to pay for twelve pa[irs] of shoes for the children of the Parish School, for which I am much obliged. —
I hope you will arrange so as to let us have some coal, for which we are in great distress. —
Very truly yours
Lucan Glebe. F. Auld.
Feb. 2d 1829. —

Plate 16: Acknowledgment of two guineas for shoes for children in parish school. Folder dated 1829 RCBL, P.0913.27

St Andrew's school drew its pupils from a wide social spectrum. Analysis of the occupation of the parents of children attending St Andrew's school from 1880 to 1914 reveals that the children of mill workers made up the majority of the pupils in the school.[55] Apart from mill workers, other occupations that featured were constable, gardener, steward, labourer, as well as gamekeeper, accountant, engineer and mill manager and clergy.[56] The wide range of occupations reflects perhaps the continuing presence of the middle classes during the second half of the nineteenth century. The major landowners of Lucan, although supporting the schools financially, did not appear to have sent their children to the local parochial schools. However, the sons and daughters of the clergy, factory and mill managers, engineers and accountants sat beside the sons and daughters of manual labourers, travellers, and herdsmen.

CLERGY AND LAITY - A UNITED FRONT

On the eve of disestablishment, the popular perception of the Church of Ireland was that it was primarily identified with the governing classes and the landowning gentry. As noted previously, the involvement of some of these elite families can be clearly traced in the life of the parish of Lucan prior to disestablishment. In order for the church to survive the separation of state and church this involvement was more crucial than ever.

Disestablishment led to an upsurge of lay involvement in the Church of Ireland, and Lucan parish was no exception. A total of fifty-six parishioners or landowners registered for the first time as vestrymen for the parish of Lucan in 1871. From this list, twelve men were elected by ballot, to serve on the select vestry of St Andrew's church. These included local gentry and owners of considerable property in the parish, including Charles Vesey of Lucan House; John Wills of Willbrook, who was a justice of peace; H. F. Colley of Lucan Lodge; and John Woodward Stanford of Ounavarra, Lucan.

Prior to disestablishment, the custom in the Church of Ireland was that a weekly collection taken up at Sunday services was used for the relief of the poor. However, expenses that before disestablishment, had been paid for out of parish cess or by the ecclesiastical commissioners, now had to be met out of this collection. These included payment to the sexton, bell ringer and organist, the purchase of coal, oil and communion wine, as well as repairs to the church. Nevertheless, a sum of money from the weekly collection was still put aside for the poor. In 1871 the vestry resolved that Elizabeth Young should be given 2s.6d. per week and Mrs Callaghan should be given 1s. per week from the offertory funds, and that a further sum 'not exceeding 3s.6d. a week be at the disposal of the clergyman and churchwardens for the relief of the poor.'[57] Subsequently the rector was given the uncontrolled distribution of 10s. per week from the offertory for distribution among the poor of the parish. This was reduced to 6s. per week in 1887 at the suggestion of the rector, who felt that 10s. was somewhat excessive, a reflection perhaps of high employment in the area.

In the decades following disestablishment, there were two occasions during the year which attracted larger than usual congregations. The collections taken up at these services were given to deserving causes. These were hospital Sunday, when the collection was given to the Dublin hospital Sunday fund (this was an annual collection begun in 1873 which was held in most Dublin churches in aid of the hospitals of Dublin), and the harvest thanksgiving festival, when the collection was divided among several deserving causes. Harvest thanksgiving was a festival that was first observed in the Church of Ireland after disestablishment and was viewed by some as evidence of a pagan influence on church worship. The harvest festival was first celebrated in St Andrew's church in 1872 and proved to be very popular, attracting a congregation of 170 people, exceeding the congregations at Easter and Christmas. The church received special cleaning before the festival and was decorated with flowers and wheat for the occasion and a guest preacher was invited to attend.

That year the collection was divided between the Irish Clergy Sons' Education Society and the Stewart Institution for Imbecile Children. The Irish Clergy Sons' Education Society, which had a school in Lucan, had been in existence since 1859 with 'the object of supplying instruction to the sons of the poorer clergy in our land.'[58] The other recipient of the collection, now called Stewarts' Hospital, situated in nearby Palmerstown, was founded in 1869 by a parishioner of St Andrew's, Dr Henry Hutcheson Stewart.[59] The same format was continued in later years with the collection divided between several different charities. In 1878 part of the collection was sent to the Dublin Prison Gate Mission.[60] This was the first time that this mission ever received a donation from a harvest offering and this fact was gratefully acknowledged in the *Irish Times* by Mrs Marcus Eustace on behalf of the mission.

There were also a number of special sermons with guest preachers held in Lucan church every year in aid of various causes including the Church Missionary Society, the parochial school, the Protestant Orphan Society and the Protestant Orphan Refuge Society. The object of the latter society was to 'preserve to our Church destitute orphans who have had one Protestant parent, being the only society in Ireland to cater exclusively for such children, as the Protestant Orphan Society did not take such orphans under its care,'[61] only taking orphans who had had two Protestant parents. The cost of maintaining an orphan in the institution, which was supported solely by voluntary contributions, was £8 per year.

In Lucan parish, there is evidence that, after disestablishment, women raised money for a wide variety of causes both at home and abroad by way of bazaars, cake sales, collection boxes and cards, reflecting perhaps the increase in philanthropy among middle class women during the nineteenth century.

During this century the Church of Ireland had a strong missionary tradition and this commitment deepened after disestablishment. Fifty years after disestablishment, although the membership of the Church of Ireland had declined, their contributions to the foreign missions had increased by nearly 500%.[62] In 1897 the Hibernian Auxiliary to the Church Mission Society was supported by 555 parishes in Ireland. In addition to the special church services held on behalf of the missions, female parishioners proved invaluable at raising funds for overseas missions.

In Lucan these included the Church Mission to Jews, the Church Missionary Society, and a woman's missionary society, the Church of England Zenana mission, whose Hibernian auxiliary was formed in 1897. The object of this society was to make known the gospel of Christ to the women of India and China.[63] Although there is no evidence of any female parishioners of Lucan becoming missionaries, the financial support provided by parishes in Ireland was considerable and enabled missionary societies to support both male and female missionaries in many countries throughout the world. Nevertheless, despite the support for overseas missions, local causes were not neglected. The ladies of the parish also collected money on an annual basis for such diverse causes as the Claremont Institution for the Deaf and Dumb, the Coombe Ragged School, the Girls' Friendly Society, Miss Carr's Home, the Ragged Boy's Home and the Church of Ireland Temperance Society and Band of Hope. This latter society was founded under the sanction of the General Synod in 1876 and promoted temperance through moral, social and legislative action.

Traditionally, church music was provided by the schoolmaster or mistress of the parish school and this was the case in St Andrew's. A considerable amount of money was spent each year on music and church psalters for the use of the choir. The choir took part in choral festivals, holding special practices on a regular basis after church service. The choir, under the instruction of the schoolmaster and organist Robert Magahy, appeared to go from strength to strength, singing at special services as well as the normal Sunday services with Mary (Polly) Cromer often taking the solo part. Lucan choir belonged to the Dublin Diocesan Choral Association, and in 1888 eighteen of the members, in common with church choirs from all over the city and county of Dublin, travelled to Dublin to attend the choral festival in St Patrick's Cathedral.

Under the patronage of Colonel C. Colthurst Vesey, the Lucan Choral Union was formed with the object of practicing sacred and secular part-singing, extending the knowledge of music and of improving and advancing church psalmody. The president was the Reverend Benson and membership was open 'without distinction of class or creed, to all who cared to avail themselves of its benefits.'[64]

CLUBS AND SOCIETIES

Church-based societies and clubs were at the height of their popularity during the late Victorian era. In 1890 the men of the parish instigated the Lucan Mutual Improvement Association. The object of the association was to foster 'a spirit of Christian fellowship among the Protestant men of the neighbourhood: all such being eligible for admission on the basis of the Apostles Creed.'[65] Meetings were held in the parochial school house on the first and third Monday during the winter months. The annual subscriptions of 1s.were used to defray expenses for light, fuel and stationery.

The rules of the association stated that all officers and committee members were to be laymen, although the association undertook a mixture of sacred and secular activities. Meetings opened with hymn singing and prayers, followed by a reading from the scriptures and a discussion of the text. Approximately forty-five minutes were devoted to this part of the meeting, following this approximately one hour was devoted to secular discussions. Members, who were permitted to bring male friends to the meetings, were encouraged to write short essays on general subjects which were read to the meeting and were followed by a general discussion of the topic. Some parishioners of Leixlip, including the rector, were members of the association, and in 1901 it was suggested that the name of the association be amended to include the word Leixlip; however, nothing came of this proposal and the name of the association remained the same, an indication perhaps that the vast majority of its members came from Lucan.

The subjects to be discussed were agreed beforehand by the committee and were extremely varied, covering such topics as tobacco and opium smoking, total abstinence versus moderation, strikes, socialism, free trade, women's suffrage, home rule, poverty, education and vivisection. Some topics caused dissent amongst members, notably James Linton's paper on marriage in 1898, in which the availability of divorce was advocated. Almost all of the men present objected to this suggestion and Linton was severely reproved for his views on marriage and told that such views could not be accepted or tolerated by the association.[66] A further cause for dissension was at a well-attended meeting in 1896, when John Woodward Stanford addressed the meeting with a paper which posed the question 'is it in our power as an association to do more for the improvement of the moral and social life of Lucan?' Stanford suggested that improvements could include the lighting of the village, and that a reading room, gymnasium, co-operative store, a band and possibly a guild, could be provided, the latter 'so that boys leaving school and passing into manhood might be well looked after.'[67] These proposals invoked much discussion during two meetings, the first meeting being devoted to a discussion on the feasibility of lighting in the village. It was felt by the meeting that street lighting for the long winter evenings would be desirable and it was decided, after a heated discussion, that a committee should be formed, which would consult with the 'leading gentlemen of the neighbourhood, including Roman Catholics, and take such further steps as may be decided upon.'[68] The other items did not find much favour among the thirty-two members present. Joseph Shackleton approved of a gymnasium being provided but thought that the notion of a co-operative stores would be a nonsense in Lucan, as was a suggestion of wash-houses when there was the river Liffey at hand.

Although women were not admitted into the association they were permitted to attend, and on occasions, to address, open meetings which were held several times a year. Jane Wigham Shackleton, wife of Joseph Shackleton who owned the nearby Anna Liffey Mills, was a much travelled lady and a keen photographer, who delivered a lecture on more than one occasion about her travels. She was accompanied on these occasions by one of her three sons who operated a magic lantern to illustrate her talks.[69] In 1903 there were moves to permit women to become members of the society. However, this did not happen and by 1904, the number of members had fallen to such an extent that reluctantly, the remaining members disbanded the Lucan Mutual Improvement Association.

Plate 17: Reverend Charles Benson and his wife Belinda Jane in the garden of Lucan rectory circa 1900 (photograph by Jane Wigham Shackleton)

Although women were not permitted to become members of the Lucan Mutual Improvement Association, during the nineteenth century other associations were formed which permitted only women members. The Mother's Union was founded in England in 1872. Initially a parochial movement in the Church of England, it was launched as a diocesan movement in 1887,[70] the same year that the first Dublin branch was founded in Raheny parish by Annabella Jane Hayes, wife of the incumbent. The Mothers' Union brought together women from differing social classes and its main aim was to uphold the sanctity of marriage. The Lucan branch of the Mothers' Union was inaugurated in 1912. The wife of the rector, Mrs Holmes Gillman, was president of the branch which had twenty-seven members. Although there is no written evidence, oral tradition has it that there was also a thriving branch of the Young Women's Christian Association in the parish at the beginning of the twentieth century,[71] an indication perhaps of the increased participation of females in the life of the parish. The common denominator of all these social organisations was their exclusiveness: they were for the parishioners and their Protestant friends only.[72]

CONDITIONS IN LUCAN VILLAGE IN THE EARLY NINETEENTH CENTURY

Although no longer a civil body, during the latter half of the nineteenth century the vestry of Lucan parish complained on many occasions both to local businessmen and to the Celbridge board of guardians about conditions in Lucan village.[73] In 1887, Hills Mills were responsible for diverting the current of the River Liffey so as to strike the south or parsonage bank. Objection was made to this and also to the nuisance caused by the erection of a privy overhanging the river and to the pollution caused by offensive matter being discharged into it.[74] These two complaints were possibly connected, as the diversion of the current probably caused the effluent from the privy to be washed up on the vestry grounds which swept down to the river at that point. This matter is recorded as being satisfactorily resolved three months later, when the mill owners resolved to move the privy and to 'shut the same with timber to the bottom.'[75]

However, it was not only church property which concerned the vestry. In 1887 a complaint was made by the vestry to the Celbridge board of guardians about the condition of the Old Hill road, and an open sewer in the village. In 1893 the vestry drew the attention of the Celbridge board of guardians to the 'extremely unsanitary conditions of some houses in Lucan,'[76] and some years later in 1897 of the 'shamefully defective water supply to the town,' and of the necessity of lighting the streets.[77] So it seems that although after disestablishment the only civil function of the parish was the obligation on the rector and churchwardens to keep a registrar of marriages solemnised in the church, the vestry of Lucan parish were still concerned about general conditions in Lucan village.

Although it was 1897 when the subject of lighting the streets of Lucan village was first discussed by the select vestry of St Andrew's Church, the matter of lighting the church was a matter of much discussion at select vestry meetings and in July 1910 the vestry decided to install gas lighting in the church and provisionally accepted an estimate of £76.13s.6d. from the Sun Gas Company of Wellington Quay in Dublin. Nevertheless, seven years later it appears that electricity came to Lucan village when the Lucan Tram Company sought permission from the vestry to erect poles for electric light wires on the parochial school premises. The agent for the company undertook to pay 1s. per pole per annum to the parochial treasurer as well as guaranteeing that the poles would be removed at his own expense should the select

Change in the population of Lucan 1831 - 1926

Year	1831	1841	1851	1861	1871	1881	1891	1901	1911	1926
Population	2772	1977	1642	1340	1395	1389	1439	1605	1641	2283
C. of I. Population	531			331	306	209	219	305	196	190

Table 1.4: Source: The Census of Ireland from 1831 to 1926 and the First report of the commissioners of public instruction, Ireland. H. C. 1835 (45 & 46), xxxiii

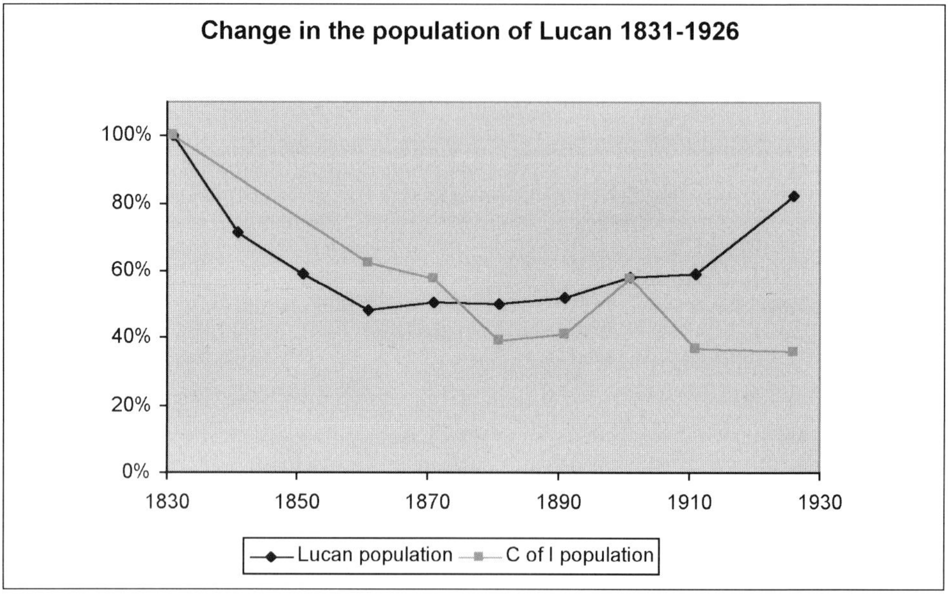

Table 1.5: Source: as above

vestry so request.[78] The rector the Revd Charles Benson subsequently decided to take the opportunity of having electric light installed in the schoolhouse as the poles were already on the premises.[79]

In Lucan, the general population increased in the period from 1911 to 1926. The Church of Ireland population however, remained relatively static during that time, losing only six members. As noted earlier, opportunities for employment in Lucan were excellent. This was especially true during the period from 1911 to 1926. Hills Mills, for example, had secured the contract to supply material for uniforms for the allied forces and the Czarist troops in the Russian revolution of 1917, thus creating additional employment for the area.

CONCLUSION

Despite the fact that the village of Lucan was a thriving community in the nineteenth century with opportunities for employment in the many mills, agriculture and in service, it is clear from the surviving Church of Ireland records that there was also considerable poverty. The civil duty of the Church of Ireland and the moral duty of its parishioners as well as the involvement of the elite in Lucan is evident from the time St Andrew's church was first built. The Vesey family, as the major landowners, were very involved both with the building of the church and the day-to-day running of the parish. In spite of the fact that during the period 1823 to 1871, Lucan parish had a succession of six different incumbents, their presence and that of the major landowner in the area had a stabilising effect on the parish.

Although, in the established church, prior to 1871, women were entitled to hold church office and to attend vestry meetings, there is no record of their formal involvement in the parish structures of the two churches of Leixlip Union. Nevertheless, the informal involvement of women is evident in Lucan where the wife and the daughter of Colonel George Vesey ensured that some of the Protestant poor (especially widows) were adequately clothed and that the children who attended the parochial school were properly nourished.

However, following disestablishment, women were barred from holding parochial office or attending vestry meetings, but female participation in parochial affairs had become more evident. Although men dominated the formal structure of the church, women now dominated its voluntary structure. Women were vital in all aspects of fund-raising for the church, and the 'ladies of the parish' through their support and practical work contributed much to Church of Ireland parishes countrywide.

Bibliography

Manuscript Primary Sources

Belfast, Public Records Office of Northern Ireland:

Minute book of the York street congregational Church mutual improvement society, 1900-14. MS CR/7/3/F/2.

Minute book of the Dorcas and benevolent society, 1912. MS CR/7/3/H/72.

Dublin, National Archives of Ireland:

Register of the national board of education, district 37, Lucan No. 2 school, 1880-1904, MS ED 2/147.

Relief commission papers, 1845, MS RLFC2/Z/1290.

Relief commission papers, 1845, MS RLFC/Z13210.

Relief commission papers, 1846, MS RLFC4/9/62.

Relief commission papers, 1846, MS RLFC4/9/63.

Relief commission papers, 1846, MS RLFC5/13.

Relief commission papers, 1846, MS RLFC5/8-5/14.

Dublin, Representative Church Body Library, Braemor Park:

Archbishops mandate for holding vestries, 8 March 1822. RCBL P.0913.27.

Letters, bills & receipts in folders dating from 1822-1832. RCBL P.0913.27.

Letters, bills & receipts in folders dating from 1860-1911. RCBL P.0913.27.

Lucan parochial infant school, 1833-55 (incorporating parish accounts 1864-70). RCBL P.0913.13.

Lucan parochial school accounts, 1851-64. RCBL P.0913.13.

Lucan parish accounts, 1891, 1913-16 & 1921. RCBL P.0913.27.

Lucan poor accounts 1850-65. RCBL P.0913.07.

Preacher books 1859-92. RCBL P.0913.08.

Vestry minute books, 1870-1957. RCBL P.0913.05.

Minute book of the Lucan mutual improvement association, 1890-1904. RCBL P.0913.28

Miscellaneous documents relating to Lucan parish 1778-1966, D. 6, Box 179 (loosely sorted by date).

Church of Ireland parish Centre, Lucan:

Vestry minute book, 1822-2008.

Co. Dublin, St Andrew's school, Lucan:

St Andrew's school female register, 1880-1960.

St Andrew's school male register, 1880-1960.

St Andrew's school observation book, 1881 –1958.

Primary Printed Sources

1st report of the Church education society for Ireland, (Dublin, 1840).

6th report of the Church education society for Ireland, (Dublin, 1846).

22nd report of the Church education society for Ireland (Dublin, 1862).

23rd report of the Church education society for Ireland (Dublin, 1863).

29th report of the Church education society for Ireland (Dublin, 1869).

D'Alton, John, *The history of the county of Dublin* (Dublin, 1838), p. 655.

Gerard, Francis, *Picturesque Dublin old and new* (London 1898).

Griffith, Richard, *The Primary Valuation of Rateable Property in Ireland, County Dublin* (Dublin, 1851).

Jordan, Thomas, *Census of Ireland 1821-1911*, i. (New York, 1998).

Lord Walter Fitzgerald, 'Patrick Sarsfield, earl of Lucan', in *Journal of the County Kildare Archaeological Society*, iv, pp 114-147 (1905).

Lee, Alfred, T., (ed.), *Church of Ireland, Journal of the general convention – first session 1870*, (Dublin, 1870).

Lewis, Samuel, *A topographical directory of Ireland*, (2 vols.) (London 1837).

Lucan parish accounts, n.p.1875-76, 1879, 1881-84, 1889-91, 1903-06, 1909. RCBL P.0913.27.

Parliamentary Gazetteer of Ireland, ii, 1844-45 (Dublin, 1846).

Salmonleap Magazine, (n.p, 1915). (in the possession of Mrs Lily Miller, Lucan, Co. Dublin).

Parliamentary Papers

First report of the commissioners on ecclesiastical revenue and patronage, Ireland, H.C. 1833 [762], xxi.

Second report of the commissioners on ecclesiastical revenue and patronage in Ireland, H.C. 1834 [523], xxiii.

Fourth report of the commissioners of ecclesiastical revenue and patronage in Ireland, H.C. 1837, [500], xxi.

Royal commission on the revenues and condition of the established church in Ireland, H. C. 1867-8 [4082], xxiv.3.

First report of the commissioners of public instruction in Ireland, H. C. 1835 [45 & 46], xxxiii.

First report of the commissioners of Irish education enquiry, H. C. 1825 [400], xii.

Second report of the commissioners of Irish education enquiry, H. C. 1826-7 [12], xii.

Appendix to the second report of the commissioners of Irish education inquiry, H.C. 1826-7 [12], xii.

A bill for the establishment and maintenance of parochial schools and the advancement of the education of the people of Ireland, H. C. 1831 (286), 1.491.

Commission for inquiry into the revenues and conditions of the established church in Ireland, H. C. 1867-68 [4082], xxiv.3.

Census of Ireland, 1831, comparative abstract, H. C. 1833, (23), xxxix.3.

Census of Ireland, 1841, abstract, H. C. 1843, [459], li.319.

Census of Ireland, 1851, County Dublin, H. C. 1852-53, [1553], xci.25.

Census of Ireland, 1851, returns of agriculture produce, part ii, H. C. 1852-53, [1589] xciii.i.

Census of Ireland, province of Leinster, 1861, H. C. 1863, [C3204], lix.i.
Census of Ireland, province of Leinster, 1871, H. C.1872, [C663], lxvii.i.
Census of Ireland, province of Leinster, 1881, H. C.1881, [C3042], xcvii.i.
Census of Ireland, province of Leinster, 1891, H. C. 1890-91, [C6515], xcv.i.
Census of Ireland, province of Leinster, 1901, H. C. 1902 [C847], cxxiii.
Census of Ireland, province of Leinster, 1911, H. C. 1912-13, [C6049], cxiv.
Census of Ireland, province of Leinster, 1926, part 1, Religion, iii. Department for Industry and Commerce, 1928.

Gazettes and Newspapers

Church of Ireland Gazette (Dublin, various dates, 1902-1918).
Irish Ecclesiastical Gazette (Dublin, various dates, 1875-1884).

Directories

Dublin directory (Dublin, various dates, 1806-1849).
Irish church directory and yearbook (Dublin, various dates, 1863-1900).
Slater, *Directory of Ireland*, 1846 (Manchester & London, 1846).
Slater, *Directory of Ireland*, 1856 (Manchester, 1856).
Slater, *Directory of Ireland*, 1881 (Manchester, 1881).
Thom's *Irish almanac and official directory* (Dublin, various dates, 1850-1921).

Secondary Sources

Acheson, Alan, *A history of the Church of Ireland 1691-1996* (Dublin, 1997).
Akenson, Donald Harman, *The Church of Ireland, ecclesiastical reform and revolution, 1800-1885* (London, 1971).
Akenson, Donald Harman, *The Irish education experiment* (London, 1970).
Atkinson, Norman, *Irish education* (Dublin 1969).
Balfour, Graham, *The educational systems of Great Britain and Ireland* (Oxford, 1903).
Bosco, Sr M. John, *Lucan old and new* (n.p., 1977).
Bowen, Desmond, *The Protestant crusade in Ireland, 1800-70* (Dublin, 1978).
Champney, Arthur, C., *Irish ecclesiastical architecture* (2nd ed., Ireland, 1970).
Coolahan, John, *Irish education: its history and structure* (Dublin, 1981).
Cox, Jeffrey, *The English churches in a secular society: Lambeth, 1870-1930* (Oxford, 1982).
Craig, Maurice, *The architecture of Ireland: from the earliest times to 1880* (Dublin, 1997).
Crawford, John, *St. Catherine's parish Dublin 1840-1900* (Dublin, 1966).
Crawford, John, *The Church of Ireland in Victorian Dublin* (Dublin, 2004).
Crossman, Virginia, *Local government in nineteenth century Ireland* (Belfast, 1994).
d'Alton, Ian, *Protestant society and politics in Cork 1812-1844* (Cork 1980).
Deane, J. L. B. (ed.), *The constitution of the Church of Ireland, Dublin*, 1978, and amendment to chapter iii & v (Dublin, 1999).

Dowling, P. J., *A history of Irish education* (Cork, 1971).

Duffy, Hugo, *James Gandon and his times* (Dublin, 1999).

Ford, Alan, McGuire, James, & Milne, Kenneth, (ed.) *As by law established* (Dublin, 1995).

Hone, Joseph, Craig, Maurice & Fewer, Michael, *The new neighbourhood of Dublin* (Dublin 2002).

Hurley, Michael, (ed.) *Irish Anglicanism 1869-1969* (Dublin, 1970).

Hutchison, Sam, *Towers, spires and pinnacles, a history of the cathedrals and churches of the Church of Ireland* (Wicklow, 2003).

Joyce, Weston, *St John, The neighbourhood of Dublin* (6th ed., Dublin,1994).

Leask, Harold, *Irish churches and monastic buildings*, 3 vols (Dundalk, 2000).

Lewis, Samuel, *A topographical directory of Ireland*, (2 vols) (London 1837).

Luddy, Maria, *Women in Ireland*, 1800–1918 (Cork, 1995).

Luddy, Maria, *Women and philanthropy in nineteenth century Ireland* (Cambridge, 1995).

Martin, David, *A general theory of secularization* (Oxford, 1978).

Milne, Kenneth, *A short history of the Church of Ireland* (Dublin, 1966).

Moody, T. W., & Martin, F. X., (ed.), *The course of Irish history* (2nd ed., Dublin, 1993).

Mulhall, Mary, & O'Flynn, Joan, (ed.) *Lucan and Lucanians* (2nd ed., Kildare, 1996).

MacCarthy, Robert, *Ancient and modern* (Dublin, 1995).

Maguire, Martin, 'Our people: the Church of Ireland and the culture of community in Dublin since disestablishment' in Gillespie, Raymond and Neely, W. G., (eds), *The laity and the Church of Ireland, 1000-2000* (Dublin, 2002).

McDowell, R. B., *The Church of Ireland 1869-1969* (London, 1995), pp 277-303.

McLeod, Hugh, *Secularisation in Western Europe, 1848-1914* (London, 2000).

Neely, W. G., 'The laity in a changing society, 1830–1900', in Gillespie, Raymond and Neely, W. G., (eds), *The laity and the Church of Ireland 1000-2000* (Dublin, 2002), pp 106–225.

O'Dwyer, Frederick, *Lost Dublin* (Dublin, 1981).

O' Keefe, Tadgh, *Medieval Ireland an archaeology* (Gloucestershire, 2000).

Patton, Henry, E., *Fifty years of disestablishment*, (Dublin 1922).

Phillips, Walter Alison (ed.), *History of the Church of Ireland*, 3 vols (London, 1933).

Purvis, Jane (ed.), *Women's history: Britain, 1850-1945* (London, 1995).

Refausse, Raymond, *Church of Ireland records* (Dublin, 2000).

Robinson Tweed, Carol, *Taney: Portrait of a parish* (Dublin, 1994).

Stewart's Hospital centenary year book (n.p, 1969).

Wallace, W. J. R., (ed.), *Clergy of Dublin and Glendalough* (Dublin, 2001).

Wheeler, H. A., & Craig, Maurice, *The Dublin city churches of the Church of Ireland* (Dublin, 1948).

Unpublished works

Donohoe, Patricia, 'The Church of Ireland Parishes of Leixlip and Lucan in the nineteenth

century' (M.Litt thesis, N.U.I. Maynooth, 2003).
Fitzsimons, Gerard Oliver, 'The Church of Ireland and disestablishment 1870-1880' (M. A. thesis, N. U. I. Maynooth, 1997).

Footnotes

1. Alan Acheson, *A history of the Church of Ireland 1691-1996* (Dublin, 1997), p. 200.
2. The Church Disestablishment Act was passed into law in 1869 and enacted on 1st January 1871.
3. W. G. Neely, 'The laity in a changing society, 1830-1900', in Raymond Gillespie & W. G. Neely (eds), *The laity and the Church of Ireland 1000-2000* (Dublin, 2002), p. 196.
4. Arthur Young, *A tour in Ireland 1776-7* (Dublin, 1779), p.706.
5. Richard Griffith, *The Primary Valuation of Rateable Property in Ireland, County Dublin* (Dublin, 1851), p. 14.
6. ibid. p. 12.
7. Samuel Lewis, *A topographical dictionary of Ireland* (2 vols) (London, 1837), pp 221-2.
8. Miriam Moffitt, *The Church of Ireland community of Killala and Achonry 1870-1940* (Dublin, 1999), p.16.
9. Sr M. John Bosco, *Lucan old and new* (np, 1977), p. 9.
10. Samuel Lewis, *A topographical directory of Ireland*, (2 vols) (London 1837), p. 321.
11. ibid.
12. Preachers' book, 1868-1872, 25 December 1868 (RCBL P.0913.08).
13. Relief commission papers (N.A.I., MS RLFC4/9/63).
14. Donald Harman, Akenson, *The Church of Ireland, ecclesiastical reform and revolution, 1800-1885* (London, 1971), p. 172.
15. John Crawford, *St Catherine's parish Dublin 1840-1900* (Dublin, 1996), p. 26.
16. Accounts, bills & receipts in folder dated 1825 (RCBL P.0913.27).
17. John Crawford, *St Catherine's parish Dublin 1840-1900* (Dublin, 1996), p. 25; John Crawford, *The Church of Ireland in Victorian Dublin* (Dublin, 2004), pp 15-16.
18. Vestry Minute Book [1822-2008],15 April 1830, Lucan Parish Archive
19. ibid., 12 April 1830.
20. ibid., 16 May 1831.
21. Alan Acheson, *A history of the Church of Ireland 1691-1996* (Dublin, 1997), p. 144; Donald Harman, Akenson, *The Church of Ireland ecclesiastical reform and revolution, 1880-1885*, (London, 1971), p. 172.
22. Correspondence in folder dated 1825 (RCBL P.0913.27).
23. ibid.
24. ibid.
25. Frederick O'Dwyer, *Lost Dublin* (Dublin, 1981), p. 94.
26. *The book of common prayer... of the United Church of England and Ireland* (Oxford,

1826), p. 195.

27. These were discovered when the organ was moved during the renovations carried out in the 1990s and are held in the RCBL.
28. Correspondence in folder dated 1824 (RCBL P.0913.27).
29. Griffith's valuation lists a widows home in Lucan under the patronage of the then curate, Reverend Hugh E. Prior.
30. Correspondence in folder dated 1824 (RCBL P.0913.27).
31. ibid., 1828.
32. ibid., 1831.
33. Correspondence in folder dated 1828 (RCBL P.0913.27).
34. V.M.B. [1822-2008], 16 June 1835, Lcn P. A.
35. ibid.
36. ibid.
37. Lucan church poor account book 1850-65 (RCBL P.0913.07).
38. ibid.
39. Preachers' book, 1859-67 (RCBL P.0913.08).
40. V.M.B. [1822-2008], 27 Feb. 1827, Lcn P. A.
41. ibid.
42. *Second report of the commissioners of Irish education enquiry*, pp 590-3, H.C. 1826-7 (12), xii.
43. V.M.B. [1822-2008], 13 Mar. 1827, Lcn P. A.
44. Lucan parochial infant school account book, [1833-5] , 20 May 1836 (RCBL P.0913.13).
45. ibid., 20 Feb. & 20 Mar. 1836.
46. The Reverend Ould to an unknown benefactor, 2 February 1829, folder dated 1829 (RCBL P.0913.27).
47. V.M.B. [1822-2008], 27 Mar. 1831, Lcn P. A.
48. *Second report of the commissioners of Irish education inquiry*, pp 590-3, H.C. 1826-7 (12), xii.
49. Parish school account book, [1851-63], 14 Sept. 1851 (RCBL P.0913.13).
50. ibid.
51. Leixlip Union of parishes includes the parishes of Leixlip, Lucan, Esker, Confey and Stacumney.
52. Parish school account book, [1851-63], 14 Sept. 1851 (RCBL P.0913.13).
53. Lucan parochial infant school account book, [1833-55], 20 Aug. 1836 -20 June 1839 (RCBL P.0913.13).
54. ibid., 18 Dec. 1841-10 June 1853.
55. School register, girls, 1880-1960, School register, boys, 1880-1960, held in St Andrew's school, Lucan.
56. ibid.
57. V.M.B. [1870-1892], 9 Oct. 1871, (RCBL P.0913.05).
58. The honorary secretary of the society, the Reverend Charles W. Benson, who was the head master of Rathmines school, preached at a charity service in aid of the society in Lucan church in 1881.

59. The association with the parishes of Leixlip Union and Stewarts Hospital continues to this day with children bringing gifts to the harvest service which are then distributed to the children in the hospital.
60. Lucan parish accounts, 1878-9, printed and hand-written accounts in folder dated 1875 (RCBL P.0913.27).
61. Unsorted correspondence in folder dated 1890-9 (RCBL P.0913.27).
62. Henry E. Patton, *Fifty years of disestablishment* (Dublin 1922), p. 311.
63. Correspondence in folder dated 1890-9 (RCBL P.0913.27).
64. Insert in back of preachers' book 1880-85 (RCBL P.0913.08).
65. Rules on inside cover of the minute book for the Lucan Mutual Improvement Association [1890-1904] (RCBL P.0913.28).
66. Minute book for the Lucan Mutual Improvement Association [1890-1904], 7 Mar. 1898 (RCBL P.0913.28
67. ibid., 16 Nov. 1896.
68. ibid., 7 Dec. 1896.
69. The magic lantern and slides are still in the possession of the Shackleton family.
70. Martin Maguire, 'Our people: the Church of Ireland and the culture of community in Dublin since disestablishment' pp 277-303, in Gillespie & Neely (eds), *The laity and the Church of Ireland*, p. 295.
71. Author's conversation with Mrs Mary Linton, Leixlip, 24 August 2003.
72. Maguire, 'Our people', p. 296.
73. Lucan came under the auspices of the Celbridge Poor Law Union.
74. V.M.B. [1870-1892], 24 Jan. 1887 (RCBL P.0913.05).
75. ibid., 30 Apr. 1887.
76. V.M.B. [1893-1913], 27 Jan. 1893 (RCBL P.0913.05).
77. ibid., 13 Oct. 1897.
78. V.M.B. [1913-57], 31 July 1917 (RCBL P.0913.05).
79. It was not until 1935 that electric light was installed in St Andrew's church.

LUCAN DEMESNE *and the* LIFFEY VALLEY
EIGHTEENTH CENTURY PASTORAL LANDSCAPE TO TWENTY-FIRST CENTURY PUBLIC PARK

by Suzanne Pegley

INTRODUCTION

The story of Lucan Manor begins as a previous essay has shown, with the granting of Lucan to the Norman Alard FitzWilliam who then transferred the lands to Wyrrys, Wyrris or Werrick Peche.[1] In the fourteenth century the lands of Lucan came into the possession of the Fitzgerald family, earls of Kildare and remained under their control until the sixteenth century. After Gerald the tenth earl of Kildare was attaindered[2] in 1554, the lands were leased to Matthew King the clerk of court. His lease however set down a few requirements which stated that he had to live there, that he spoke only the English tongue and that he dressed in the English manner. The final provision stipulated that he would have no communication with the Irish. While this would appear on the surface to be rather awkward since he was living in Ireland, what this meant was that he should have no contact with the landed Anglo-Norman Irish, the old English families, who were rather troublesome.

THE SARSFIELD AND VESEY FAMILIES

Some years later in the early seventeenth century the lands of Lucan came into the ownership of Sir William Sarsfield of Dublin.[3] Originally the Sarsfield's had arrived in Ireland as standard bearers with Henry II in 1175. By the sixteenth century the family had prospered and John, the younger son of Roger Sarsfield, the family patriarch, became in 1531 the Mayor of Dublin. John was succeeded as mayor by his eldest son Patrick in 1553 and by Patrick's second son William in 1566. It was this William who was conferred with a knighthood by Sir Henry Sidney, Lord Deputy of Ireland, for his services against Shane O'Neill, and was seneschal of the Royal manor of Newcastle in 1591.[4] It was during this period that he acquired the

Manor of Lucan and the lands at Tully Castle, Co. Kildare and, looking into the future, he was the great-great grandfather of the Jacobean General Patrick Sarsfield, Earl of Lucan.[5]

Directly prior to the Civil War in England, a rebellion occurred in Ireland in 1641, by-and-large a rebellion of the Old English Catholic community, lead by Rory O'Moore and tacitly supported by the Palesmen.[6] Patrick Sarsfield, (hereafter the elder) grandson of Sir William, was, by the nature of his landowning, a Palesman. Having allowed his two estates of Lucan and Tully, Co. Kildare to be used by the conspirators he was expelled in 1642 from the Irish House of Commons for High Treason.[7] The subsequent Cromwellian conquest saw the dispossession of the Old English nobility and the defeat of the Catholic cause.

During the Cromwellian period 1649-1653, the Sarsfield family were forced to forfeit their lands at both Lucan and Tully to the Commonwealth government. The Sarsfield family, consisting of Patrick, his wife Ann O'Moore, daughter of the leader of the 1641 rebellion, and their five children were assigned an estate in Mayo. After the Restoration, Patrick pursued the return of their lands at Lucan and Kildare but was deemed complicit in the rebellion. Despite his demonstrable loyalty, by allowing the Royalist forces to use Lucan as a base from which to attack the commonwealth positions in Dublin, the claim for restoration was denied. A rather unfortunate situation, penalised for whatever stance he took.[8] The case went to the courts for adjudication and in the detail of the claim it was declared that despite Patrick's apparent guilt, his wife Ann and their son and heir William, then aged eleven,[9] were innocent and William therefore had the right to inherit after his father's death.[10] Thus began the lengthy struggle to retrieve the lands at Lucan, awarded to Sir Theophilus Jones in the intervening years. Rather an opportunist, Jones had at first supported the Commonwealth, and then later became active in the restoration of Charles II.[11] The court's finding against Sarsfield was to Jones' benefit because it was not considered just to remove him from the Manor of Lucan, awarded to him for his royalist allegiance, without finding him somewhere else equally prestigious. Jones celebrated the outcome of the trial and it was 'many years before all the Sarsfield property was surrendered to them.'[12]

In 1663, in what seemed a ruthless act, the elder Patrick's second son William declared his father a papist and demanded the restoration to himself, of some seventy-nine parcels of land. Sir William, the father of Patrick (the elder) had died coinciding with the crisis of 1641, and in his will he had left his estate to his son Patrick who duly took over the lands of his inheritance. However, these lands would be confiscated under the Cromwellian Confederacy, and, after the restored monarchy, awarded to Sir Theophilus Jones. Although William was subsequently declared the rightful heir to his grandfather Sir William's estate in 1673, he was unable to take up residence in Lucan due to Jones' status.[13]

Plate 1: Patrick Sarsfield (? – 1693)

In 1671 William Sarsfield married Mary Stuart, the sister of James Scott Duke of Monmouth and Buccleuch (1649-1685), believed to be the natural daughter of Charles II, by Lucy Walters.[14] The marriage was arranged with a view to securing the king's influence as William sought to regain Lucan. However, according to the Sarsfield papers, Charles II, rather than reinstate the land, instead gave William £200.00.[15] Four years later having applied pressure on Jones to sell his interest, an agreement was finally reached to exchange other lands for the immediate possession of Lucan by William.[16] The king would provide the alternate lands provided William settled £800 per annum on his wife Mary. This would appear to confirm a concern for Mary if not an acknowledgement of her as his daughter. However, before these negotiations were signed and sealed William died, having provided his wife with only a £200 lump sum, and once again Jones refused to give up Lucan Manor. As the rightful if not the defacto owner of Lucan, William on his death in 1675, determined in his will that, firstly his two sons should inherit and if they did not survive, his younger brother Patrick Sarsfield would inherit. William's daughter and his two sisters were only to inherit if everyone else died. Jones continued to hang on, despite added pressure arranged by the king, awaiting the results of Mary Sarsfield's efforts, now married to William Fanshawe, to secure Lucan for their daughter Charlotte. In 1683 Patrick (the younger, future Earl of Lucan), in order to strengthen his claim to Lucan, proved the will of his grandfather (Sir William) with the result his father Patrick (the elder) became the defacto owner of the Manor of Lucan. However, with the death of Jones a year later in 1684 the situation was finally resolved and the last obstruction to the Sarsfield restoration was removed.[17]

Patrick Sarsfield (the younger) (plate 1) was a well known figure during the Williamite period of Irish history. The third son of Patrick Sarsfield (the elder) he was born around 1655. There were three possible birth places for him; Lucan, Tully or Mayo, none of which are more compelling than the other. Wauchope contended that his upbringing was at Tully Castle. Any myths, he maintained, that connected Patrick's childhood to Lucan were simply that, myths.[18] He married Lady Honora Burke[19] in 1689, daughter of the 7th Earl of Clanricarde, 'a woman of impeccable Irish pedigree', far grander than the Sarsfields.[20] In 1690 Ireland happened to be the location for the battle that was to decide who would succeed to the throne of England, William of Orange or James II, his father-in-law. Patrick headed a strong force guarding Athlone against the forces loyal to William of Orange. Sarsfield, despite being deemed incapable of taking overall command of the army, was given the responsibility of Commander-in-Chief of the forces in Ireland for five months at the beginning of 1691. Later that year he acted in the same capacity for a further four months.[21] Following the siege of Athlone the Duke of Tyrconnel travelled to France and, on his return, brought with him a patent from King James II, creating Sarsfield Earl of Lucan, Viscount of Tully, and Baron of Rosberry, in recognition of his dedication and in May of 1691 he was made Colonel of the Lifeguards.[22] He died on the battle field in France in 1693. Patrick and Lady Honora's son James Francis Edward, second earl of Lucan, spent his life on the continent and, in 1719, died unmarried, aged twenty six, and for the time being the title was extinct.[23]

Although the title earl of Lucan, of the first creation, ended with the death of Patrick's son, the Sarsfield connection continued with Lucan for many more years. As mentioned above this association centered on the continuing dispute of the inheritance of Lucan Manor. After the death of Jones and following the death of his two little nephews, William, the youngest at the age of three and Charles at age eight, Patrick obtained title to the Lucan property, circa 1684 then valued at £2000 per annum.[24] However, when Patrick, because of his connection with James II, was attaindered subsequent to the Siege of Limerick in 1691, the lands of Lucan were lost to the family once again.

Consequent to Patrick Sarsfield's death in 1693, the lands at Lucan were again in limbo. There were however three women to consider; the two sisters of Patrick and William, Ann and Frances as well as William's daughter Charlotte. Although the two sisters' status had been settled following their father's death in 1675, when their grandfather's will was proved, their yearly allowance from the estate was now frozen. Charlotte's position remained legally uncertain and her mother continued to work to have her daughter's inheritance rights resolved.[25]

Charlotte meanwhile, after her father's death, had married Agmondisham Vesey, the son of John Vesey, Archbishop of Tuam, and his second wife Ann Muscamp. His half brother was Sir Thomas Vesey Bishop of Killaloe and Ossory, from whom the Viscounts de Vesci are descended.[26] This was not the first connection of Vesey's to Lucan, they previously appeared in connection with Lucan in the Crown Calendar Documents in 1297 in which lands of Kildare were surrendered. The unnamed widow Vesey, who received compensation for the forfeiture of her husband, also unnamed, was described as receiving 'homage and service of Ralph Pypard of the manors of Salmon Leap', among others; an early and direct connection to the lands within the greater Lucan area granted to Wyrris de Peche.[27]

Agmondisham, whose curious name comes from his maternal grandfather Colonel Agmondisham Muscamp,[28] became a spirited campaigner after their marriage for Charlotte's rightful inheritance of Lucan. Although Agmondisham was exhausted by the length of time it took to secure his wife's rights and the benefit to their daughters, as can be seen in the Sarsfield papers, he never gave up and finally in 1696 King William III reinstated the lands of Lucan to them. On her death, in 1699, he sought the succession rights for their two daughters Ann and Henrietta.[29]

Plate 2: Lucan House; Shackleton Collection

The restoration was finally secured by an act of parliament during the first year of Queen Anne's reign in 1702.[30]

Now that the land had been secured and there was evidence of an income the two daughters of Agmondisham and Charlotte Sarsfield, could benefit from the value of the estate. As a result their marriage prospects were greatly enhanced, as Jane Austin would later show in her novels. Ann married Sir John Bingham of Mayo, a cousin, and their son Charles, in the second creation of the title in 1795, became the first Earl of Lucan.[31] In the 1719 marriage settlement between Ann and Sir John, it appeared that her father, Agmondisham, purchased from her half of the Lucan estate for the sum of £2,000, which included a yearly annuity or allowance of £250. Provisions in the will of Sir John's late father, Sir Henry Bingham, provided an additional £250 annuity and consequently she received £500.00 per annum.[32] Agmondisham was then in a joint ownership of Lucan Manor with his second daughter Henrietta.

After the death of Charlotte, Agmondisham Vesey married Lady Jane Butler. Their first son was named Agmondisham, once again the ancient Surrey surname being used as a first name.[33] This child would ultimately be the main beneficiary of his father's dedication to his first wife's rights of inheritance. Agmondisham (jr), like his father before him, bought his half sister Henrietta's share of the estate when in 1721 she married Caesar Colclough of Moccorry and Tintern Abbey, Wexford. Couched in legal language, it appeared that he acquired from Henrietta her lands at Lucan and Tully, Co. Kildare for £5,000, in the form of a fifteen year mortgage.[34] Agmondisham died 23 March 1738 and Lady Jane, in restoring the old church of St Mary's adjacent to the manor lands, erected a memorial to her 'dearly beloved husband' and with whom she was interred in 1746.[35] With the death of his father Agmondisham (jr) inherited the other portion and thus he became the sole owner of Lucan Manor and the lands in Kildare.

Agmondisham (jr), as a man of his time and, as was the fashion, transformed the lands of Lucan Manor – with the discerning sensibilities of his wife Elizabeth – into the pastoral landscape of Lucan Demesne that his father had begun. He was also, like many other aristocratic land owners, an amateur architect and as a recent book on Lucan House showed, he was also quite an able architect.[36] The original castle had been improved and added to soon after his marriage[37] and later in 1772 this was removed and a new house built, described by Mark Bence-Jones as a Palladian villa.[38] The house (plate 2) as it stands today was based on Vesey's own refined ideas and the interiors were inspired by the leading interior designers of the time; William Chambers, James Wyatt[39] and two pupils of Chambers, Edward Stevens and John Yenn, may also have been involved. During this period James Wyatt was advising on Abbey Leix, the home of Agmondisham's brother-in-law Sir John Denny Vesey, 1st Baron Knapton, whose descendants would become the Viscounts de Vesci, and one can easily see how ideas would have moved from one house to the other. To those who have tried to unravel the architectural genius of Lucan, in particular John Redmill, the definitive connection between the various individuals named above regarding Lucan House remains uncertain.[40] Recently however Conor Lucey in his timely book has shown Michael Stapleton's involvement in the plaster work.[41] Vesey himself received praise from no less a figure than William Chambers who was impressed by Agmondisham's 'new method of slating'[42] and, adding to the accolades, Arthur Young praised the grounds surrounding the house.

> 'The house is rebuilding, but the wood on the river, with walks through it, is exceedingly beautiful. The character of the place is that of a sequestered shade. Distant views are every where shut out, and the objects all correspond perfectly with the impression they were designed to raise: it is a walk on the banks of the river, chiefly under a variety of fine wood, which rises on varied slopes, in some parts gentle, in others steep; spreading here and there into cool meadows, on the opposite shore, rich banks of wood or shrubby ground. The

walk is perfectly sequestered, and has that melancholy gloom which should ever dwell in such a place. The river is of a character perfectly suited to the rest of the scenery, in some places breaking over rocks; in others silent, under the shade of spreading wood.'[43]

Agmondisham (jr) became the Right Honourable Member of Parliament first for Harristown, Co. Kildare and later Kinsale, Co Cork,[44] accountant general of Ireland from 1762, privy councilor in 1776 and was named Professor of Architecture of Doctor Johnson's Utopian University.[45] As to what type of person he was, a biography of his wife Elizabeth Vesey described him as an intellectual lightweight who was chronically unfaithful. Although as a casual acquaintance he was good company, few valued his advice or friendship possibly because of his tendency to follow fashion.[46] All of which showed him in a rather negative light.

ELIZABETH VESEY

The Right Honourable Agmondisham Vesey married Elizabeth Vesey (plate 3), a young widow of taste and refinement, c.1746, his first cousin and second daughter of the late Sir Thomas Vesey.[47] Her first husband, Mr William Handcock of Willbrook, Co. Westmeath had died in 1741.[48] Elizabeth was described as small in stature, charming and flirtatious who beguiled both men and women's friendships and retained her beauty for many years. Mrs Mary Delany the diarist, a close friend, gave her the name 'Sylph' due to her wit, spirit and vivacity. As to her marriage, Elrington Ball drops a tantalizing comment

Plate 3: Elizabeth Vesey by unknown artist; circa 1770.
© National Portrait Gallery, London

that while Agmondisham and Elizabeth may not have had the most ideal of marriages 'notwithstanding some difference in taste, which became more accentuated in later life, she found him a kind indulgent husband.'[49] And in another passing comment 'Mrs Vesey's idiosyncrasies were not those to which every man would have accommodated himself'.[50] These very subjective comments reflected the attitude of the time: women should be supportive and allow men to take the lead in society.[51]

Elizabeth's correspondence, despite her notoriously bad handwriting, was received as delightful entertainment; with an enchanting style, flitting from one topic to another in flights of fancy, which was treasured by the recipients.[52] Elizabeth Vesey was part of a group of intellectual and literary women, largely based in London in the 1750s and 1760s, who became known collectively as the Bluestocking Circle.[53] The circles, as a collective, were concerned with 'defining a model of public life that incorporated the political, the intellectual and the sociable.'[54] Throughout the eighteenth century social life could be somewhat dissolute and frivolous. Receptions of the Bluestocking Circle, attended by the leading intellectuals of the day, both male and female, were primarily intended for women and devoted to what Angelique Day described as 'rational conversation'.[55] Elizabeth's salons included such significant literary women as Frances Boscawen, Elizabeth Carter and Elizabeth Montagu who was her close friend, and were of immense significance to the society of the time. Leading male intellectuals who also attended the salons in London and Bath were Samuel Johnson, Sir Joshua Reynolds, Richard Sheridan and Horace Walpole, the son of the late prime minister.[56] The Shakespearian actor David Garrick and his wife also attended, as well as the young novelist Fanny Burney.

Elizabeth's literary parties in London in the 1770s and 1780s, before Agmondisham's death, were extremely successful and were described by Walpole, a lively social commentator, and 'lifelong epicure of gossip'[57] as 'babels', apparently a complement. Notions of self and personal identity, separate from the public displays of position and status, were developing in the eighteenth century and at the forefront of this was Elizabeth Vesey. The home in the eighteenth century for the aristocratic and upper classes was not 'in any simple sense a private domestic sphere. Genteel families were linked to the world in a multiplicity of ways, [these links were] expressed through a variety of encounters that took place in the home'.[58] The 'feminization' of culture was characteristic of the period, where women played a civilising role in the area of commerce and politics.[59] Their assemblies, centred securely in the domestic sphere, nevertheless appealed to a wider extra-political circle and 'defined by egalitarian sociability, conversation, and the advancement of civic virtue [that] relied on an essentialist and exclusive understanding of gender.'[60] Although with hindsight the Bluestocking Circle may be considered feminist they did not regard themselves as inheritors of a feminist tradition. Any women who had been writing in the late seventeenth and early eighteenth centuries were not within the cannon of work that the Bluestocking women would have been aware.[61] Their influence would come from a variety of writers contemporary to themselves who began to develop the idea of the condition of women in society that included education.[62]

Interaction on these different levels extended to Lucan and was very likely the reason that Agmondisham and Elizabeth Vesey and the Dean and Mrs Delany found so much mutual enjoyment in each other's company. At the Vesey's various houses in both Ireland and England Elizabeth created a blue room for her Bluestocking Circle to meet and at Lucan the very fashionable Wedgwood room could have been the location for her literary evenings.

MRS DELANY

Mary Granville Delany, who regularly visited Lucan, wrote about its beauty, the walks and follies and described the social activity. Mary Granville, widowed in 1724, married Dr Patrick Delany in 1743. When Patrick was appointed dean of Down they came to live in Ireland at Delville, close to Glasnevin, and for the remainder of his life, some twenty four years, they lived mainly in Ireland. Through the publication in 1991 of the Irish material in Mrs Delany's diaries and letters, it was apparent that the Veseys were close friends. She and Elizabeth had previously met on a visit to Ireland in 1731 when Elizabeth was married to her first husband.[63] From her diary of the mid 1740s, Mary Delany described how, with both of them remarried, they were regularly meeting for breakfast, occasionally joined by Emily Countess of Kildare and others.[64]

Mrs Delany displayed a great fondness for the company of both Elizabeth and Agmondisham and the demesne at Lucan. In February, June, October and December of 1750 there were four visits to Lucan, accompanied by Dr Delany, recorded in her diary and three that included breakfast. The entries though brief give us an insight to the demesne and a view into the nature of the Vesey's lives.

The first reference to Elizabeth Vesey in Mrs Delany's diaries occurs in relation to a journey that was underway in February of 1750 to Lucan. About a mile from their destination the Delany's met the Vesey's in their chariot coach and four and the two vehicles stopped. Mrs Vesey protested that they should go on as intended and that there was nothing pressing in town that she could not do another day and she would join them in their carriage. Despite little room she 'flew out of the chariot into our chaise ...... and Mrs Vesey nestled herself in so cleverly that we trotted away to Lucan everyone declaring they had room enough.' Mrs Delany's young niece however had to sit on the Dean's knee to make space available.[65]

The second reference was to the demesne which they had begun to enhance.

'17 June 1750

I spent a very agreeable day at Lucan with the Vesey's; they are improving it greatly- it is really a very sweet agreeable place and well planted.'[66]

On another occasion when the Delany's travelled to Lucan accompanied by three other friends. The popular illusion of the pastoral in the eighteenth century was evident with the early morning setting of breakfast.

'30 June 1750

Found breakfast prepared for us in Mrs Vesey's dairy, and the table strewed (sic) with roses.'

Later, when additional visitors had departed, they dined in the antechamber of the cold bath. This folly, at a distance from the house of about ten minutes undemanding walk, was on that day accessed by transport.

'...the coach carried us and brought us back to the house for tea and coffee. They are pretty people to be with, no ceremony, everybody does what they please.'[67]

'20 October 1750

Yesterday, to Lucan to breakfast with the Vesey's: it was clear and pleasant, and the autumn scene rich and beautiful, and in no place it appears with more beauty than at Lucan- the banks of the river covered with wood.'[68]

The next mention of the Vesey's demonstrated that they were decorating their home themselves, and enlisting visitors to help, almost as an afternoon amusement. It also served to show that Mrs Delany felt secure from crime in this country area.

'10 December 1750

We had a pleasant jaunt on Saturday. Went to Lucan to breakfast, found Veseys up to the chin in business, hanging pictures and settling other decorations: all of us engaged in their business, staid [sic] to dinner, and till seven in the evening, came home by charming moonlight. A comfortable circumstance belonging to this country is, that the roads are so good and free from robbers, that we may drive safely any hour of the night.'

It was evident too that it was not unusual to enlist the help of friends to improve the interior decoration of the house and in another entry she described a pleasant afternoon. Although Mrs Delany would not 'invent' her cut flowers for a number of years cutting out paper and prints was a popular pastime.

'11 June 1751

The pleasantest party I make out of my own villa is to Lucan; it is a delightful

> place, and its owners perfectly agreeable in their own house, always busy, and have some work or other to set one to do. The last time we were there, which was last Friday, Mrs Vesey had a whim to have Indian figures and flowers cut out and oiled, to be transparent, and pasted on her dressing-room window in imitation of painting on glass, and it has a very good effect: we go again next Friday to finish what we began last week.'[69]

It was apparent too that the Vesey's also visited Delville. In this entry it was clear that their leaving created a void.

> '16 March 1750/51
> Monday, the Veseys have left us and we are dull as cats and mute as fish.'

During a period when the Delany's were experiencing some legal difficulties Mrs Delany valued her friendship with Elizabeth Vesey and she wrote, highlighting the regard the two couples held toward each other, and the soothing effect of the demesne.[70]

> '26 August 1952
> We came here [Lucan] on Tuesday to dinner. There is no house in Ireland I like so well to be in for any time except my own. Mr and Mrs Vesey are very friendly and perfectly easy, so we have no sort of restraint, but say and do just what we like; but I had no great inclination to come. I had begun to dead colour my picture, and am not much now entertained with company but Dr Delany thought it would amuse me to come to this pleasant place, and as it happens I am glad we did.'[71]

The following month they stayed five days with the Veseys and although the weather was not good even caught indoors they were quite content.

> '2 September 1752
> We staid [sic] at Lucan from Tuesday till Saturday, the weather too bad to enjoy that fine place in perfection; but it is as agreeable within doors as without- perfect ease and freedom, and books and prints innumerable. I would have been glad to see nobody but themselves but that was impossible.'[72]

After the death of her husband, in 1768, Mary Delany did not return to Ireland however she continued to move in the bluestocking set and in c1777 she mentioned meeting Elizabeth when attending an evening circle.[73] In time Elizabeth Vesey's own letters[74] may throw more light on her friendships with, among others, the Lennox sisters.[75] Never-the-less even without a deeper knowledge of her letters it appeared she was part of a social milieu in Ireland that regarded the development of parklands to be of great interest and the influence of these friendships may have been reflected in the improvement of Lucan Demesne.

Elizabeth Vesey and Patrick Sarsfield were the only individuals of real national significance connected with Lucan. Although he is of interest from a military history point of view it is she who provided an inspiration for the newly developing ideas of private and public social convention. While these ideas were developed in the eighteenth century they are being reappraised in the twentieth and twenty-first centuries and Elizabeth's pivotal role is emerging.[76]

After 1782 the Vesey's did not return to Ireland preferring instead to live in England. However, only a few years later, in 1785, Agmondisham died and as the couple had no children, the lands of Lucan Demesne passed to his nephew George Vesey. Following Agmondisham's death Elizabeth became depressed to find that in his will, instead of providing for either herself or Miss Handcock her sister-in-law, he had left £1000 to his mistress. Elizabeth had been a devoted wife, despite Agmondisham's short comings, and 'maintained the façade of a successful marriage'. She had nursed him through bouts of epilepsy but depended on her circle of friends for support.[77] Elizabeth's depression increased, due in part to financial concerns, and she suffered with impaired memory, which became particularly serious after the death, in 1789, of Miss Handcock who had acted as companion and housekeeper.[78] Elizabeth Vesey died in 1791.

George Vesey born in 1761 was the grandson of Agmondisham Vesey (sr) and Lady Jane Butler and son of their second son also named George, married to Letitia.[79] George Vesey married Emily La Touche, daughter of David La Touche, of Marlay Park, in 1790, and together they had a daughter Elizabeth. Meanwhile Emily's sister, Harriet La Touche, had married into a Cork family by the name of Colthurst. Not unusually the two families were joined when Sir Nicholas and Lady Harriet's son Sir Nicholas Conway Colthurst married Elizabeth Vesey in 1819. This type of interfamily marriage that connected wealth, power and influence was quite typical within the ruling ascendancy. When Elizabeth, as an only child, inherited Lucan Demesne technically the Vesey's connection came to an end, because she and her family were Colthursts. However, in this social milieu, name change to reflect inheritance was the norm. Her second son Charles Nicholas switched his third and last names around to continue the Vesey tradition as Charles Nicholas Colthurst Vesey. This arrangement, with regard to inheritance provisions to the second son, is referred to as the cadet inheritance, the major inheritance and titles, if any, going to the eldest son. If the cadet family line should die out the material portion of house and lands, return to the possession of the main family branch.[80]

LUCAN AND THE COLTHURST FAMILY

Elizabeth Vesey and Sir Nicholas Conway Colthurst, 4th Baronet of Ardrum, Co Cork had four sons and a daughter. The first son, named George after his grandfather, married Louisa Jane St John Jefferyes, whose family owned Blarney Castle and Demesne and in 1829 became the 5th Baronet. The Cork branch of the family appears to have been in regular residence at Lucan Demesne. Evidence of this is the birth record of their daughter, Emily Frances Colthurst in the parish at St Mary's, Leixlip in 1822 and in her marriage record to George Augustus Bayly, that took place in 1851, at St Andrew's church Lucan, and where her residence was given as Lucan House.[81] The second son Charles, as mentioned previously, would inherit Lucan Demesne however, the third and fourth sons were also closely linked to Lucan. Robert Colthurst the youngest brother, who died in London in 1864; at the age of thirty-four, left in his will £2,000 for the erection of a convent for the Mercy Sisters in Lucan. He and his elder brother David La Touche Colthurst had both fought in the Crimean War and were so impressed by the self-sacrifice of the Mercy Sisters on the battlefield that they vowed to convert to Catholicism. However, the Sisters, regarding Lucan as outside their sphere of interest, declined the offer and instead it was taken up by the Presentation Sisters who were interested in the education of children. In 1867, with land donated by Edward Quigley, David La Touche Colthurst saw that his brother's wishes were carried out.[82] David died in 1907 and a memorial plaque to the two brothers was placed in the Roman Catholic church of St Mary's in Lucan.[83] This plaque and Edward's headstone beside the new parking lot behind St Mary's, may indicate that the two men did convert, giving up their protestant affiliation.

Charles Nicholas Colthurst Vesey, following his marriage to Ann Fraser in 1858, and the births of their four children, seemed to have secured the future inheritance of his estate. The children were George Colthurst, born in 1859, Charles Nicholas in 1860, Edward Robert in 1862 and a daughter whose name and birth date is not known.[84] However, of the three sons, one died in his thirties, and none married. Mrs Mary Cecilia Hatch was mentioned in Edward Robert's will, as executrix and his 'sole next of kin', but was not a beneficiary.[85]

The elder son, Capt. George Colthurst Vesey of the Shropshire Light Infantry, died aged thirty-five in June 1894, during an outbreak of bubonic plague, while on active duty in Hong Kong. The outbreak lasted from May until September of that year. For his heroic service he received the Hong Kong Plague Medal. The War office authorized the awarding of the medal 'in recognition of the exceptional services rendered in stamping out the recent terrible plague there, whereby the regiment lost one officer and six men...'[86] The one officer was George Vesey and his gold medal was sent to his mother (plate 4).

Plate 4: 1894 Hong Kong Plague Medal

The remaining two brothers died within two years of each other both aged fifty-five, Charles Nicholas in 1915 and Edward Robert, the youngest son, in 1917. With their deaths the estate of Lucan Demesne passed back to the main branch of the Colthurst family, Barons of Ardrum and owners of Blarney Demesne. Through the wills of the two brothers glimpses of their assets and responsibilities were revealed. In 1903 Charles Nicholas leased the Constabulary Barracks in Lucan to the Board of Works for a term of sixty years. In 1909 he acquired seventy-one shares in the Dublin and Lucan Steam tram Company and in 1915, the year of his death, he was listed as Director. Although his assets amounted to £23,460, with Brazilian and Chilean bonds accounting for £2,488, his list of creditors diminished the capital sum considerably. In his list of outstanding debits, a significant amount, £1746.16.6, was owed to a successful local building contractor, John Cromer. Further debits and funeral expenses reduced the sum to only £6,807. Under the terms of his uncle David La Touche Colthurst's will, his personal legacy to the total of £5000 was to have gone to his aunt, Francis Drummond Colthurst, a resident of Bournemouth; however she had died in 1911 and it appears that the monies were then divided between her three daughters.[87]

Charles Nicholas died in a nursing home in London and payment to that establishment was shown in his list of debits.[88] His brother Edward Robert died in 1917, in a Manchester nursing home; however, his assets were not as substantial. He died possessed of a gold watch, £2000 and outstanding debits that included £181 for John Cromer.[89]

The possession of Lucan Demesne then returned to the main branch of the Colthurst family to Richard St John Jefferyes Colthurst, the eldest son, to whom it presented a convenient financial solution. Born 1887, Richard would succeed his father as 8th Baronet of Ardrum in 1955, but in the 1920s he was a man concerned with the eventual inheritance of his title and lands. He and his wife, Charlotte Cholomonsey, were the parents of two daughters but, pragmatically, in an attempt to produce sons, Sir Richard decided on a second marriage. As a consequence, on the advice of his solicitors, he sold Lucan Demesne in 1925 to establish a divorce settlement.[90] The parents of his first wife had agreed to settle on their daughter a sum of £30,000; the sale of Lucan was undoubtedly meant to reconcile the arrangement.[91] The following year he married Denys West daughter of Augustus William and Maida West of Leixlip House, Co Kildare and with her had two sons Richard and George.

THE AUCTION OF LUCAN HOUSE AND DEMESNE

The sale of Lucan House and Demesne, on the instructions of Captain Richard St John Jefferyes Colthurst, took place on 14 July 1925.[92] The sale held at the auction rooms of James H. North at 110 Grafton Street was handled by Colthurst's solicitors Messers Barrington & Son of Ely Place. The sale also included the 'attractive first class residence' of Ounavarra, which sits on the hill above Lucan Demesne and was built either in the late eighteenth or early nineteenth century.

Lucan House and demesne were sold as one unit that contained just over forty six acres. Five further lots amounted to slightly more than 230 acres. (fig. 1) The first lot consisted of the house, Ounavarra, with over eleven acres. The second lot, with parts of the two townlands of Coldblow and Laraghcon featured a small gate lodge, and was bounded by half the Liffey on the southern side and contained over thirty-six acres. The third lot, which involved parts of St Catherine's Park and Coldblow, was also bounded by half the Liffey on the southern side and the weir and amounted

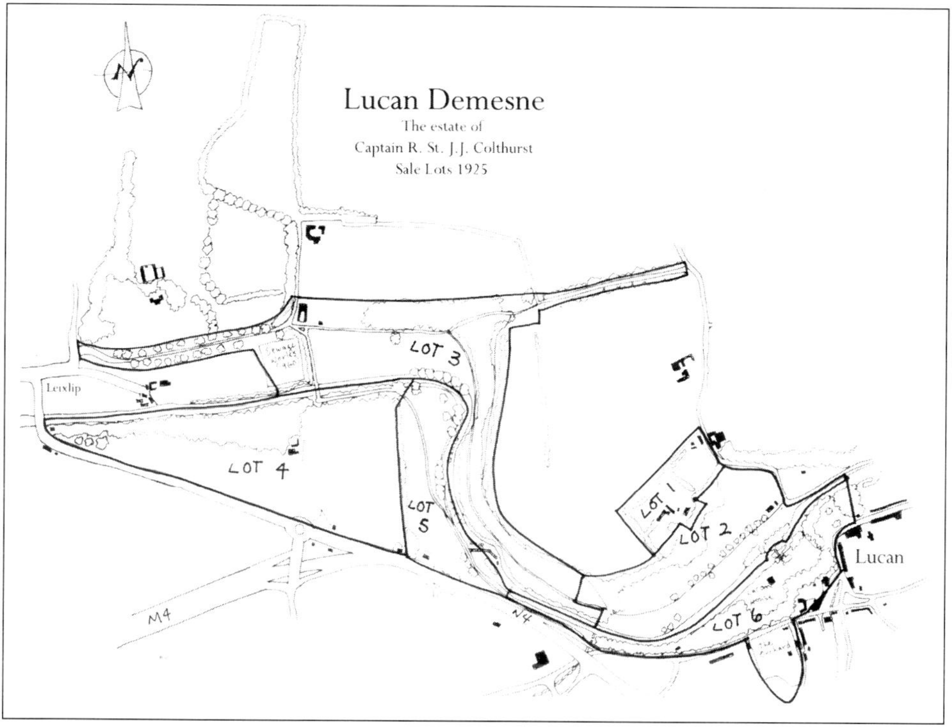

Figure 1: Auction Lots, Lucan Demesne, Sale Catalogue 1925. NAI – redrawn by S. Pegley in combination with modern maps

to over forty-five acres. The fourth and largest lot of eighty-five acres covered parts of the townland of Lucan Demesne with the main Lucan/Leixlip road as its southern boundary and half the Liffey as the northern border. The fifth lot of thirty acres contained the cottage orné, which the sale catalogue related romantically as the cottage where Patrick Sarsfield had hidden after being attaindered for treason. It was probably built sometime in the mid-eighteenth century by Elizabeth Vesey.[93] The southern border was again the county road and the northern was the Liffey, which in this section included a small island and the weir. Most of the lands for sale in the first five lots were described either as ornamented, containing valuable timber, in grass, tilled or suitable for building. Some used all of these elements to describe the potential to the purchaser.

The sixth lot was Lucan House, described in the sale catalogue as the Manor House. The surrounding land, of approximately forty six acres, included parts of the townlands of Lucan Demesne, Coldblow, Lucan and Pettycannon and, like two of the other lots, the northern boundary was formed for one-third of a mile by half of the Liffey. The description of the house stated it was in the Grecian style that today would be accepted as the Palladian or Georgian style. The setting was romantically portrayed with an account of a small tree-covered island in the river in the proximity of the house. Finally, with the mention of central heating and electric light, it was evident that the building had been brought up to modern standards.

Interior Description

The sale catalogue went on to list the attributes of each of the six main rooms on the ground floor. The entrance hall: lofty and well proportioned about thirty-six by twenty-four feet, intersected by scagliola columns, stucco cornice and frieze, with a mantelpiece of Siena marble. The square drawing room: twenty-four square feet elaborately decorated in Italian stucco work. The oval drawing room: thirty-three by twenty-four feet with the walls decorated in the Adams' style. The dining room: thirty-five feet by twenty-four feet contained a ceiling of elaborate Italianate stucco work with five raised panels.[94] The library: twenty-four feet square with antique curved statuary marble fireplace. Although doubt has arisen today it was thought at the time that the embellishments in the entrance hall and the square drawing room were by Angelica Kaufman and this information was included in the catalogue. The bedrooms, kitchens, servant accommodation, out offices and stable yard were all positively mentioned. The grounds were depicted as being 'ornamented by old timber and planted with choice varieties of trees and flowering shrubs.' It was also revealed that access to the walled garden was via a tunnel under the county road. This garden appears to have been a kitchen garden with a peach house and [grape] vinery.[95]

AUCTION OF THE CONTENTS

Any researcher who has the good fortune to come across an inventory or auction catalogue of the object of their study has a far greater insight into the lifestyles of their subject. Goods play a role in defining how individuals define themselves. By looking at the items listed an idea of the attitudes and ideas, on the part of the subject family, can emerge because it is through possessions society elevates, imitates or differentiate themselves from others.[96] In particular it is the pastels by Hugh Douglas Hamilton mentioned below that define the owners of Lucan Demesne as consumers of a social level of high sophistication. The inclusion of Chippendale and Sheridan furniture also supports this view.[97]

Two months after the house and lands were sold the contents of the house were auctioned over a three day period, beginning on 29 September, at Lucan House.[98] The catalogue illustrated that the family had amassed some significant furniture and pictures throughout the eighteenth and nineteenth centuries. In the dining room were fourteen Adam's style mahogany chairs and sideboard. The sideboard sold for 820 guineas and the chairs for £112, both considerable sums for the period. In this room were four paintings by Thomas Roberts showing Lucan Demesne, at the height of the pastoral landscape gardening epoch in the eighteenth century, as created by the Rt Hon Agmondisham Vesey. These paintings today form part of the state collection in the National Gallery of Ireland. Sadly the notes in the catalogue did not include the prices they achieved.

In the drawing room two pairs of Sheraton demi-lune card tables sold for 48 and 18 guineas respectively and the Sheraton cylinder-top writing table for 65 guineas. There were two other Sheraton pieces that went for more modest sums. The sum of 56 guineas was paid for a Collard and Collard 'boudoir' grand piano which appeared to have been one of three musical instruments in the sale. The other two were spinets rather ignominiously being used in bedrooms as writing and dressing tables.

In the oval drawing room, the significant paintings collected by the family were mainly by Hugh Douglas Hamilton, an important pastellist and painter of the eighteenth century. A number of his major paintings are in the National Gallery in Dublin. The Vesey and Colthurst family, and their friends, were portrayed by Hamilton in some thirteen pictures. Typically his pastels are small, set in oval frames, and twelve appear to fall into this category however, the size of the final double pastel was not given. Hamilton's other double portraits are the same size as his single portraits, and perhaps this was also true here. Portraits listed, relevant to this study, included husband and wife George and Emily Vesey, her parents David and Lady Cecilia La Touche, and in the double portrait Lady Colthurst and Mrs Jefferyes. The Hamilton pastel that achieved the highest price was the portrait of Emily's sister

Elizabeth La Touche which realized 70 guineas. The others mentioned reached an average of 38 guineas each. Other artists featured in the collection were T. Hone and Adam Buck. Of the china in this room there were a number of Sevres items, a Worcester floral tea service and a blue and white Wedgwood classic vase. Josiah Wedgwood, who opened a shop in Dublin in 1772, created a consumption phenomenon with his pottery and it was not surprising that such an item was to be found at Lucan House. Charles Bingham the first earl of Lucan (of the second creation) was, according to recent research, an ardent Wedgwood collector.[99]

In the library, among a considerable number of items, were Chippendale tables; one a writing table and one a 'sunk-top' table, a pair of fold-top card tables and finally an 'Old Irish' rent table, the latter sold for £124. A two drawer, three tier, fretwork bracket was also in the Chippendale style. In this room were displayed a number of paintings but only two are relevant, an unattributed portrait of Charlotte Sarsfield, wife of Agmondisham Vesey, and another of her father William Sarsfield credited to William Wissing (1656-87). These two paintings were the oldest recorded in the catalogue, since William and Charlotte both died in the late seventeenth century.

The description of the entrance hall with the tiger's head and tiger skin rug, combined with Carrara marble font, complete with entwined serpent handles on a plinth, had a distinctly Victorian feel. Reading the list of furniture in the adjacent rooms and viewing the rooms today would suggest that they were furnished beyond their capacity, a Victorian tendency. The bedrooms upstairs held their share of significant Chippendale and Sheraton furniture, chests of drawers and mirrors as well as a number of commonplace paintings and etchings.

In the period before the major sale of 1925, Richard had already begun to sell off the lands in the proximity of Lucan Demesne and a number of small parcels of land were sold in 1919 to John Cromer. The transaction in lands continued up until 1925 when the entire property was finally put up for sale. Documents show that John Cromer purchased Lucan House and portions of the Demesne at the time of the sale for £4,000.[100] He also paid the balance of the rent due on the lands he had been grazing, which brought the price to £4,676.[101] The Cromer family always believed that the house had been sold to him at a knock down price, because of debts incurred by the Vesey family for work done. However, the Colthurst family, who have been most helpful in the research of this study, are confident that it was not 'given away'. As has been shown above, Richard Colthurst sold the Demesne for his own personal reasons.

John Cromer, known as 'The Boss', carried out his business, with his brothers, in Lucan where the company continued to operate until 2006 as Cromer Brothers. John Cromer, who did not live in Lucan House, and never married, sold on the house, in 1931, to Charles O'Conor. Regularly referred to as The O'Conor Don, it was however his two elder brothers, and later his son, who successively held the family title.[102] Bence-Jones does not mention Cromer and stated that Richard St John Jefferyes Colthurst sold Lucan House in 1932 to Charles O'Conor.[103] Cromer held on to a significant portion of the demesne selling to O'Conor only the park surrounding the house, and the portion that extended down to the mill stream, where it enters the Liffey, immediately east of the Spa Hotel. In 1947 Sir William Teeling, MP for Brighton,[104] who had married the eldest of O'Conor's seven daughters, Mary Julia in 1942, first leased the house to the Italian Government for use as their embassy. Later, in 1954, the year following her death, he sold the property to them freehold. Since then it has become the residence of the Ambassador and the embassy office has moved into Dublin. Nevertheless the embassy sign remains on the pillar of the main gate sometimes causing confusion. The lands of the demesne, which remained in the possession of the Cromer family, were slowly sold off with the significant portion going to Dr Brendan Senior, who was involved with agricultural research. Presently only a very small sector remains in possession of the family. The Italian government, since they acquired their portion of the demesne, has been very responsible with the care of both the house and parkland and the house in particular is in very good repair. Had they not become the owners this may not have been the case as many great houses through lack of finance or willful neglect were lost in the 1950s and 1960s. The concern over the loss of so many houses was one of the reasons why, in 1958, the Irish Georgian Society was founded by the Honourable Desmond Guinness and his first wife Mariga Guinness.

CREATION OF PASTORAL PARKLANDS

In Claude's landscape all is lovely- all amiable- all is amenity and repose;- the calm sunshine of the heart.[105]

Pastoral landscapes are perhaps the most enduring symbol of English national identity. Given that Ireland's ruling ascendancy class saw themselves to all intents and purposes as English, the Irish landscapes necessarily also fell into this category. The spatial arrangements of the landscape that surround the great houses were therefore a political statement. That elitist and political statement has now been diluted by time and the old parklands have become an accepted vision of rural values.[106]

Initially gardens were highly structured with artificial patterns but as the eighteenth century progressed, the tendency was to become more natural. This managed wilderness was a reflection of the new relationship with the land. The sublime beauty of ideal nature, defined by the erudite and elitist, those with the most elevated minds, raised landscape to the level of art. The sublime was contrasted to the mere beautiful being the basis for the strongest emotions which the mind was capable of feeling. By allowing the sublime to be the product of emotion Edmond Burke in his essay's opened the experience to all levels of society not only those of higher sensibilities.[107] The natural unpopulated countryside was seen as spiritually uplifting and in particular pristine hill areas were seen as mystical. Powerscourt, deep in the Wicklow Mountains, would have been the classic example of the ideal nature or wilderness garden popular at the time. The enjoyment of private parklands was not limited to the landowners and their friends, indeed the public, with some control and in small numbers, were welcome to wander about the created landscape. In a highly structured social order they also knew to keep their distance from the house and withdraw if those with a perceived higher station in life were in the vicinity.

Lucan Demesne, although small, would have contained all that was essential for the fundamentals of eighteenth century parkland. The improvements of the Manor lands began with Agmondisham (sr) and one of the important steps in creating the utopian pastoral landscape required the removal of all intrusive views. In many of the great parklands in both Ireland and England this necessitated the sweeping away of whole villages to be rebuilt elsewhere. In the more modest surroundings of Lucan Demesne Agmondisham (sr) in his enhancement of the demesne had only one outstanding irritation, the position of the main road. The road, as it passed out of the village, travelled almost directly in front of Lucan House to access the bridge across the Liffey. The option to build a wall to screen the road may have been a consideration but this would have reduced the prospect from the front of the house and instead Agmondisham decided to relocate the road entirely. To facilitate its removal he organised the building of a new bridge, immediately beside the weir, and moved the road. Swift wrote a couplet, popular at the time, which indicated the perception of his munificence by which the arrangement was received by the general population.

> Agmondisham Vesey out of his bounty
> built a fine bridge.
> At the expense of the county.[108]

As the map shows, before Agmondisham (sr) moved the road the original bridge was directly opposite the curve in the old road, just before it begins the assent of the hill to Clonee, much closer to the house. The new bridge was located where the modern apartments overlooking the Liffey now stand. By comparing the map of 1760 (plate 5) and the map of 1900 (plate 6), opposite, one can contrast the positions of the old bridge and the later bridge of 1814 with the accompanying road changes.

Today, generally speaking, people aspire to create a garden in the immediate surroundings of their homes. This desire to create a green space, to simply admire, depending on the available area, economics and inclination, is now part of the domestic garden large or small. The creation of pastoral parklands around aristocratic homes led to an acceptance by society that beautiful surroundings, with references to other places and other times, was an important part of their lifestyles. By recreating the experiences of the Grand Tour this was also a way of demonstrating the sophistication attained on the lengthy period spent abroad and equally the money spent. The display of art collected during the tour in the form of painting and sculpture, a portion of the latter to adorn the parkland, also spoke of classical knowledge. The Rt Hon. Agmondisham Vesey, in his design decisions, would have no doubt been influenced by work at Carton and to a lesser extent at Castletown with the development of those parklands. References were made by Mrs Delany to Agmondisham and Elizabeth Vesey, socialising with Emily Countess of Kildare and, as Malins has shown in his examination of Delany's correspondence, Mrs Delany herself also took an avid interest in landscape design.[109] The group may also have included Katherine Conolly, who was responsible for significant tree planting at Castletown in the 1730s and 1740s, and who would have been living there until the time of her death in 1752.[110] One could surmise that gardening and estate improvement would have been a subject of conversation and from one of her letters it can be seen that Elizabeth Vesey was actively embellishing the Lucan Demesne, and showed her self-consciously eccentric side:

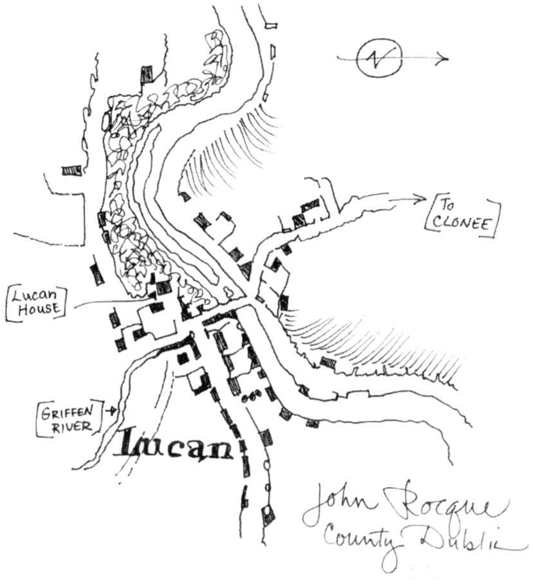

Plate 5: John Rocque. County Dublin, 1760; detail of Lucan by S. Pegley, 2008

Plate 6: Phoenix Maps, 1900, detail of Lucan

27 February 1778
"...yesterday being very cold & Trees to plant I sat in the Chaisse [sic] without horses a candle to keep me warm & a book to read while the work was going on." Later in the same letter, she refers to "the rivulet upon the banks of which I was planting a thicket."[111]

Although Lucan Demesne was by no means as large as the nearby estates of Luttrellstown, Carton, and Castletown the same principals of space, vista and ornamentation would have been employed. Finola O'Kane has written about the development of eighteenth century parklands and the significance of the Liffey Valley, describing it as the drawing board of the Ascendancy and 'an established route of colonial power and control'.[112] Beginning at Palmerstown, large parklands swept down to the river and following on, toward Lucan, most outstandingly, is the estate of Luttrellstown on the south side with St Edmondsbury on the north. Upstream from Lucan Demesne was St Catherine's, now gone. Continuing on to Leixlip, the castle commanded a site above the Salmon Leap then, within a short distance,

Plate 7: Picture of Cottage Orné, with kind permission of Desmond FitzGerald, Knight of Glin

Plate 8: Sarsfield's Monument; source: Desmond Guinness, Lucan House (Dublin, 2005)

Castletown at Celbridge with the ornamented river walks followed by the riverside walks of Celbridge Abbey. Further upstream, past Celbridge, there is Killadown and notably Straffan House that together created a flowing imagery along the course of the Liffey that was not accidental. Duffy refers to other developments of well planted landscapes along the Liffey valley from Ballymore Eustace to Leixlip naming among others; Brannockstown, Castle Martin, Millicent, Castle Browne, Rathcoffey, Lyons, Ardrass and Westown. Evidence of the remnants of the planted improved landscapes in the modern day can be seen by using Alexander Taylor's map of 1783, as a reference for plantations of trees on improved estates.[113]

The planting of the landscape and the adjustment of one landscape to view another was part of the unified concept but other aspects in the parklands were part of the pastoral illusion. One structure in a landscape can provide a point of reference to another and in the case of Lucan this could have been provided by a number of objects in the park. There was a cottage orné, (plate 7) now gone, which stood west of the house above the river, and afforded a view of the weir. A significant funeral urn (plate 8) dedicated to Patrick Sarsfield the Earl of Lucan, commissioned by the Rt Hon. Agmondisham and designed by James Wyatt, previously stood in a wooded clearing along the main Lucan/Leixlip road but has now been placed nearer the house. In order to view objects in the park a vista was cut or planted so that even from a distance they would remain visible. However there is no evidence on maps or in the alignment of trees of a large vista at Lucan Demesne. The nature of the parkland so tightly constrained by the river and the road would have prohibited the creation of a vista so it is perhaps not surprising that one cannot be discerned today. Nevertheless there was every possibility that the banqueting hall, built onto the cold bath and described below, may have been visible from the back of the house. During the earliest period of its creation in the 1750s the size of the newly planted trees would have allowed an adequate view of the landscape so perhaps it was not considered. The original position of the Sarsfield Monument did however have its own melancholy glade within a planted woodland.

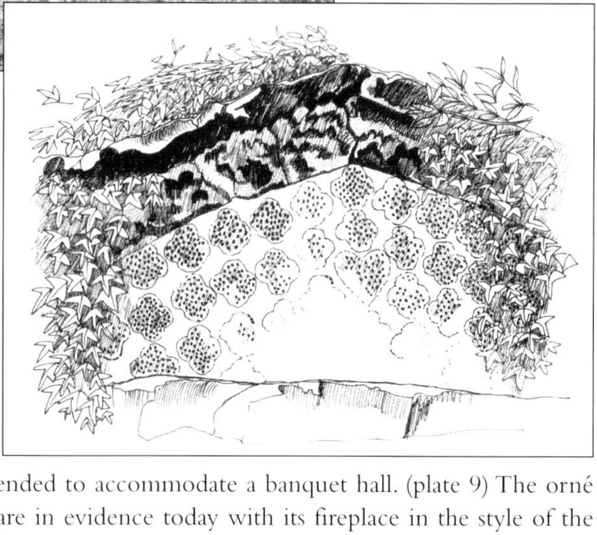

Plate 9: Banquet Hall/Cold bath; inset, detail; drawing by S. Pegley

This building, or folly, its position now considerably obscured by the trees, was at first simply a covered pool then later at the time of the Rt Hon. Agmondisham it was extended to accommodate a banquet hall. (plate 9) The orné qualities of this building are in evidence today with its fireplace in the style of the seventeenth century designer Batty Langley and the rusticated exterior. Ball wrote that the building was originally an oratory dedicated to St John and fed by a holy well.[114] The cold bath is certainly fed by a spring and may be of ecclesiastical origin but there is no tradition of a holy well associated with the site within living memory. Another structure whose ecclesiastical origins formed the medieval nucleus of Lucan is the ruined church of St Mary and its residential tower. Restored in the

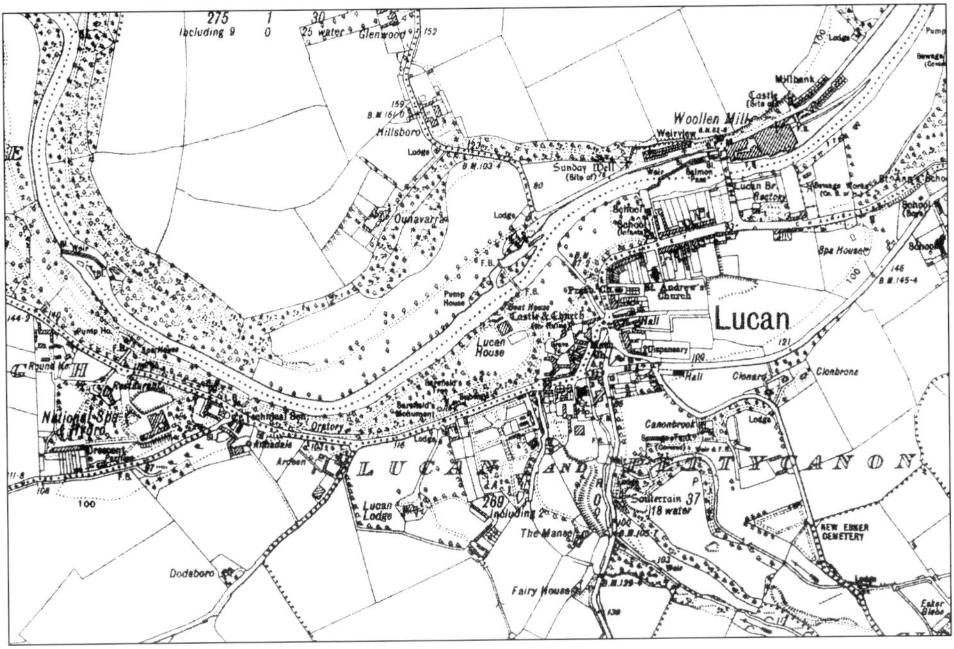

Plate 10: Ordnance Survey 1837 of Lucan area

eighteenth century it is located close to the main gate within the parkland, which provided the ideal protection for the survival of earlier landscape features.[115] These structures, and the house itself, would have been part of the view enjoyed by three smaller estates that are located on the hill above the demesne, Primrose Hill, Lucan Lodge and Canonbrook where at the end of the eighteenth the architect James Gandon lived. Indeed the Lucan area proliferates with small villas scattered about which are today largely engulfed by new houses. The map of 1837 reproduced here of the Lucan area shows their location. (plate 10) The sulphur spa, close to the river, was first discovered in 1758 and enclosed in a structure, now gone, proved very popular as a healing bath.[116] A tunnel, from the purpose-built hotel and ballroom on the opposite side of the road, at the furthest extent of the town, provided access to the bath.[117]

Another feature, this time in the river, was the weir shown by Thomas Roberts in his paintings of c. 1771 which still exists today and continues to hold back the river. Mrs Delany was so taken by the prospect that she also drew its picturesque position on the river. (plate 11) The water, held back by a low stone abutment, is directed down a chute to the benefit of modern canoeists. The importance of the river concerning the transport of goods was of serious consideration to Agmondisham Vesey and he joined with others to establish the Liffey Navigation Company. The

Plate 11: Drawing of upper Lucan Demesne weir by Mrs Delaney, 1752; source Angelque Day (ed) Letters from Georgian Dublin (Belfast, 1991)

establishment of this company would be worthy of future research since little is known about its function. A point to note however was that the banks of the river were walled, from the present sewage works in Leixlip to slightly past the first bend in the river downstream, this would have been a significant undertaking and was very likely tied up with the navigation company.

Tree Planting

The planting of specimen trees escalated in the second half of the eighteenth century and became part of the capital of an estate and descriptions of trees and ownership of their use became a feature in the deeds of houses. An example of this was seen in those of a leasing arrangement of the Deer Park of St Catherine's, in the next townland.[118] Deer parks were a distinctive feature of parklands and a quintessential symbol of wealth and prestige.[119] The leasing document stipulated that timber, standing and growing on any part of the lands and premises could not be cut down or be carried away by the leaseholder Daniel Marston, without permission. The owners, Mrs Trench and her son, in this case had placed Arthur Guinness in the position of responsibility for the trees.[120] What the nature of his involvement in the arrangement has not been established but he may well have acted as land agent. His father, Richard Guinness, had acted in this capacity for his employer the Archbishop of Cashel, Dr Arthur Price. The cutting or taking away of wood from parkland or other designated land was deemed a criminal offence in 1722. After that year it became the most common crime in the countryside.[121] If the ordered landscape of the country house parkland represented a virtuous agricultural husbandry then the planted trees 'confirmed the power of property'.[122] The avenue of trees leading up to the great houses was in particular part of the language of power and order imposed on the landscape.

In the second half of the eighteenth century both the Irish parliament and the Royal Dublin Society offered incentives to plant trees and this period represents the 'climax phase' of tree planting and between 1766 and 1806 the Royal Dublin Society granted premiums for 55 million trees.[123] Part of the planting was of selected native hardwoods trees that were seen to be characteristic of the ruling hegemony and a patriotic symbol. Oaks it was claimed were venerable, patriarchal, stately, guardian and quintessentially English. They represented the nature of the landowners and increased in status as the parklands became more natural with the evolution of gardening styles.[124] Lucan Demesne abounds with oak and, judging by their size, most were planted over 200 years ago. Other significant trees that were considered worthy of planting were beech and elm. Beech, not native to Ireland, vied with the oak for stateliness and grandeur and the elm was favoured for its' representation of the working countryside. Wordsworth began his poem 'The Excursion' with the words 'The joyful Elm/Around whose trunk the maidens dance in May.'[125] Avenues of beech or oak trees were a symbol of power over the landscape and, by inference, of society. The ordered planted trees in the landscape creating vistas or pleasing clumps were arranged to emphasize or enhance the actual extent and unity of the estate and indicated 'a military sense of command.'[126] Orchards were also part of the tree planting development and represented a potent symbol of the new culture of the high regard for trees and their conservation.[127] The demesne had a substantial orchard cum kitchen garden situated on the opposite side of the main road, accessed by a tunnel, between Primrose Lane and The Ball Alley pub. New apartments partially occupy the area, appropriately named The Orchard.

Tree planting trends began to change at the end of the eighteenth century when the broadleaf species were giving way to coniferous. By the mid-nineteenth century the ratio had shifted in favour of coniferous by 6:4. This change is reflected in Lucan Demesne with larch, Scots pine and Norway spruce growing along both sides of the river. New varieties of broadleaf trees were also being planted through out the Kildare region overlapping no doubt into Co. Dublin, the beech, mentioned above, along with the very popular ash as well as larch, horse chestnut, monkey puzzle, elm, limes, hollies and other kinds of pine and oak. Smyth sees these mini-arboreta as museum pieces of tree planting fashion.[128] The great oaks bordering the riverside walk, giving way to other broadleaf types and conifers at times, were enjoyed by the public until well into the 1960s; however, the demesne was then closed and the riverside walks became overgrown and inaccessible.

The walks were part of an avenue or drive that threaded through the whole demesne. The first section of the avenue, immediately after the main gates, with a random planting of trees rather than an avenue, branches as it approaches the area in front of the House. One branch diverts to the imposing stables and the other continues to the house. Both branches, having served their main function, continue

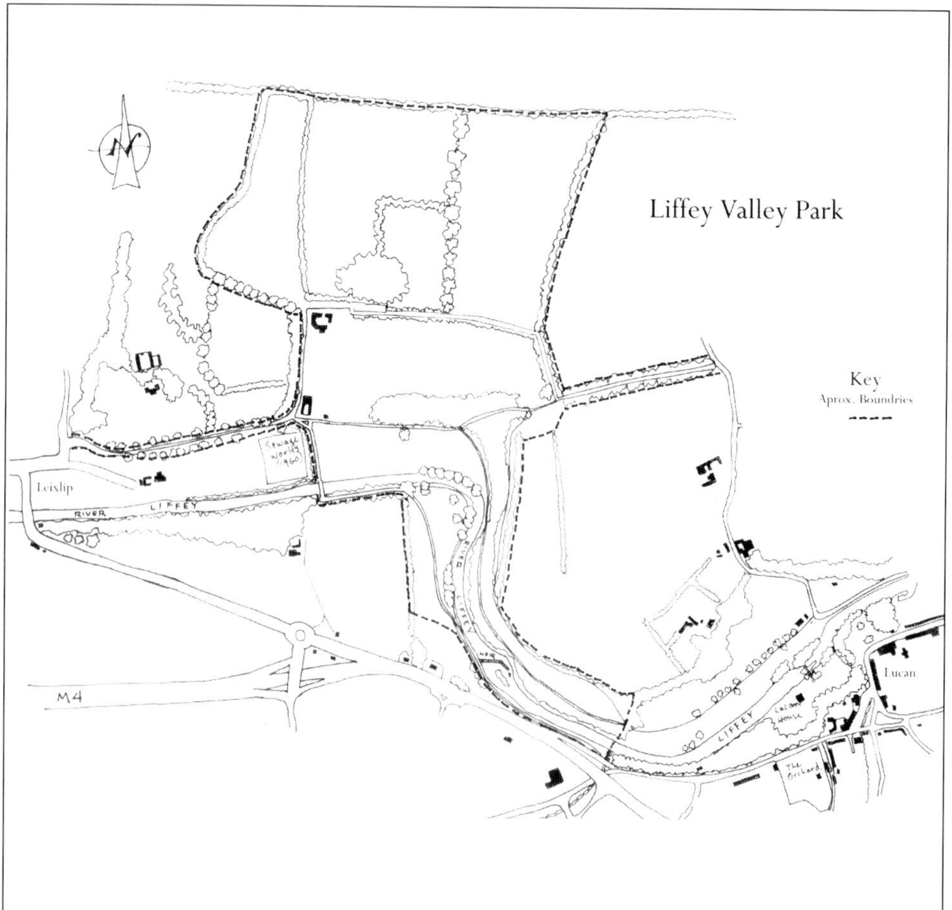

Figure 2: Liffey Valley Park; compilation of modern Ordnance Survey maps by S. Pegley, 2008

on to form what might be walking paths or alternatively rides. One passes along the river the other through the wood and the glade which contained the Sarsfield monument. As shown above, Mrs Vesey's breakfast party was transported by carriage on this drive, to and from the dairy. Both drives meet again at the narrowest point up stream from the house and carried on as one to the furthest end of the park which for the final portion passed close to the river. The end of the demesne was marked by a gate lodge opposite the Salmon Leap Inn.[129] In 1996, at the instigation of the local residents, spearheaded by the late Professor Valentine Rice, Declan Kenny and Kieran Hickey the suggestion was put to the government that they purchase the portion of the Demesne then being offered for sale by the Senior family. With the economy on the upswing the government of the day acquired the land consisting of lots three and five shown earlier. Also part of the sale was a farmyard, with a complex of buildings at the top of the hill, which includes a castellated mill, and a number of large fields that have been developed for public amenity. (fig. 12) In 1960 when the new sewage works were built Dr Senior had the county council install a bridge when they brought water pipes across the Liffey. This gave him access to his lands on both sides of the river and the ongoing agricultural research in connection with UCD, thus allowing present day walkers to avail of all areas of the public park. In the portion of the demesne that remained in private hands, the house, under the protection of the Italian government, is being maintained and is not at risk either structurally or developmentally at the present time, however one cannot predict how long that situation may last.

CONCLUSION

In the twelfth century Lucan Manor was a significant reward to an ally in victory and was apparently worth fighting for in the case of Mary Sarsfield and later Agmondisham Vesey. In the nineteenth century it was inherited by a second son who would have been more than satisfied with the park and the quality of the house. Its lack of national importance was more than compensated for by the location, close to the city yet in the country, and in a spa town full of activity and social interaction.

Lucan Manor, once beyond the city boundaries, has now been subsumed into the conurbation of an ever growing suburban sprawl. The surrounding townlands that once comprised the whole no longer look to the core of Lucan for material necessities. Lucan House which once represented wealth and authority is now without relevance to those who live and work in the area and indeed many do not know of its existence. Improved in the eighteenth century with taste and refinement by Agmondisham and Elizabeth Vesey, it is the demesne that is of the greatest significance to the present population of Lucan and Leixlip. As a public amenity the parkland, straddling the Liffey, is once again being used by individuals, groups and families to enjoy the trees planted so long ago and to delight in the flow of the river with its wildlife and the interplay with the weir. With the heightened awareness of the importance of green spaces the state is committed to maintaining this park and thus its future continuance is assured. The demesne has become a more egalitarian place where everyone may enjoy the mature results of the Vesey's concept of a romantic rural idyll, an oasis in the increasing urbanisation of the Dublin area.

Bibliography

Primary Sources

Manuscripts:

National Archives of Ireland, Sarsfield Vesey Papers.

National Library of Ireland, de Vesci Papers.

Representative Church Body Library, Registers of the Parish of Leixlip Union.

Secondary Sources

Aalen, F. H. A., Whelan, Kevin and Stout, Matthew, (eds), *Atlas of the Irish Rural Landscape* (Dublin, 1997).

Baird, Rosemary, *Mistress of the House Great Ladies and Grand Houses 1670-1830* (London 2003).

Toby Barnard, *A guide to sources for the history of material culture in Ireland, 1500-2000* (Dublin, 2005).

Toby Barnard, *Making the grand figure, lives and possessions in Ireland 1641-1770* (London, 2004).

Bence-Jones, Mark, *A Guide to Irish Country Houses* (Dublin, 1988, reprinted 1996).

Cosgrove, Denis E., *Social formation and symbolic landscape* (London, 1998).

D'Alton, John, 'Sarsfield's Horse' *Illustrations, historical and genealogical of king James Irish Army list* (1689) vol. ii (Dublin, 1855), pp 131-140.

D'Alton, John, *A History of County Dublin* (1838) (Dublin, 1976).

Daniels, Stephen 'The political iconography of woodland in later Georgian England' in Denis Cosgrove and Stephen Daniels (eds), *The Iconography of Landscape*, (Cambridge, 1988, 2nd edition, 2000), pp 43-82.

Day, Angelique, (ed.), *Letters from Georgian Ireland, Mary Delaney 1731-1768* (Belfast, 1991).

Dooley, Terence, *The Big Houses and Landed Estates of Ireland* (Dublin, 2007).

Duffy, Patrick J., *Exploring the history and heritage of Irish landscape* (Dublin, 2007).

FitzGerald, Brian, *Lady Louisa Conolly* (London, 1950).

Guinness, Desmond, *Lucan House* (Dublin, 2005).

Guinness Desmond and Ryan, William, (eds), *Houses and Castles of Ireland* (Dublin, 1971).

Hayden, Ruth, *Mrs Delany her life and her flowers* (London, 1980, reprint, 2005).

Heller, Deborah, 'Subjectivity unbound: Elizabeth Vesey as the Sylph in Bluestocking correspondence' in Nicole Pohl & Betty Schellenberg (eds), *Reconsidering the Bluestockings* (San Merino, 2003), pp 215-234.

Llanover, Lady, (ed.), *Mrs Delany at court and among the wits, being the record of a great lady of genius in the art of living* (London, 1925).

Lee, Sidney, 'Elizabeth Vesey' *Dictionary of National Biography*, vol. lviii (London, 1899), pp 289-290.

Lucey, Conor, *The Stapleton collection: designs for the Irish neoclassical interior* (Tralee, 2007).

Malins, Edward, 'Mrs Delany and landscaping in Ireland' *Irish Georgian Society* vol. xi, nos

2 & 3, (1968), pp 1-16.

Malcomson, Anthony, *The pursuit of the heiress* (Belfast, 2006).

Mills, James, 'The Norman Settlement in Leinster- the Cantreds near Dublin, *Journal of the Royal Society of Antiquaries,* vol. xxiv-xxv 1894-5, p 170.

Meigon, Anna, 'Biographical sketches of principal Bluestocking women' in Nicole Pohl & Betty Schellenberg, (eds), *Reconsidering the Bluestockings* (San Merino, 2003), pp 25-38.

Mulhall, Mary (ed.), *A History of Lucan* (Naas, 1991).

Mulhall, Mary (ed.), *Lucan and Lucanians* (Naas, 1996).

Mulhall, Mary and O Flynn, Joan (eds), *Treasures of Lucan* (Naas, 2001).

O'Kane, Finola, *Landscape design in eighteenth century Ireland, mixing foreign trees with the natives* (Cork, 2004).

Pegley, Suzanne; Donohoe, Patricia; Twomey, Valerie; Curran, Linda; *Aspects of Leixlip* (Dublin, 2001).

Schnorrenberg, Barbara B., 'Elizabeth Vesey c.1715-1791' in H.C.G. Matthew & Brian Harrison (eds), *Oxford Dictionary of National Biography*, vol. lvi (Oxford, 2000), pp 390-01.

Sweetman, H.S.,(ed), *Calendar of Documents relating to Ireland*, (London, 1881) no. 481, Close, 26 Edward I, m 9-8 dors., 22/1/1297.

Smyth, W.J., 'The greening of Ireland- tenant tree planting in the eighteenth and nineteenth centuries' in *Irish Forestry* 54 (1997), pp 55-72.

The Medals Year Book (London, 1995).

Tillyard, Stella, *A royal affair George III and his scandalous siblings* (London, 2006).

Taylor and Skinner *Road Maps of Ireland* (Dublin, 1777 & 1778), (Shannon, 1969).

Vickery, Amanda, *The gentleman's daughter, women's lives in Georgian England* (London, 1998).

Wauchope, Piers, *Patrick Sarsfield and the Williamite War* (Dublin, 1992).

Wauchope, Piers, 'Patrick Sarsfield, Jacobite first earl of Lucan' in H.C.G. Matthew & Brian Harrison (eds), *Dictionary of National Biography from the earliest times to 2000*, vol. xlviii (Oxford, 2000), pp 993-996.

Young, Arthur, *A tour in Ireland* (1776-1779), Arthur W. Hutton (ed.) vol. i (London, 1892).

Website

O'Conor Don, Wikipedia. http://en.wikipedia.org/wiki/o'conor_don, viewed 10 September 2007.

Early Leighs of Wales, Biographies, Lucy Walters. www.leigh.org/genealogy/biographies/lucywalter.htm, viewed 9 December 2007.

The Medals Book. www.lightinfantry.org.uk/Regiments/ksli/shrop_hongkong.htm, viewed 8 March 2007.

Photographs

The Banquet Hall – Suzanne Pegley.

Lucan House – Jane Wigham Shackleton c 1925 with kind permission of Mrs Mary Shackleton.

Illustrations

Elizabeth Vesey with permission of the National Portrait Gallery, London (NPG 3131).

The Cottage Orné with permission of Desmond Fitzgerald, Knight of Glin.

Drawing of upper weir Lucan Demesne by Mary Delany 4 September 1752 from Angelique Day (ed.), *Letters from Georgian Ireland* (Belfast, 1991), p. 45.

Patrick Sarsfield, earl of Lucan, unknown artist.

Footnotes

1. James Mills, 'The Norman Settlement in Leinster - the Cantreds near Dublin, *Journal of the Royal Society of Antiquaries in Ireland* vol. xxiv-xxv 1894-5. p 170.
2. Attainder (1580) To convict of a crime or dishonour [i.e. treason].
3. The first Sarsfield deed of Lucan Manor is dated 1625. Sarsfield /Vesey Miscellaneous Papers (Sarsfield/Vesey Papers, National Archives of Ireland).
4. John D'Alton, 'Sarsfield's Horse' *Illustrations, historical and genealogical of king James Irish Army list* (1689) (Dublin, 1855) vol. ii, p. 134. (D'Alton, *Illustrations*).
5. There is a question of the legitimacy of the title conferred by James II and because of this the second creation of the title in 1795 was designated the 1st Earl. D'Alton, *Illustrations*, p. 136.
6. The Palesmen: The name coined in the late sixteenth century designed to describe the section of the Old English Catholic community which lived within the heart of English rule in Ireland.
7. Piers Wauchope, *Patrick Sarsfield and the Williamite War* (Dublin, 1992), p. 5.
8. ibid., p. 5.
9. Francis Elrington Ball, *A History of the County of Dublin; The people, parishes and antiquities from the earliest times to the close of the eighteenth century*, Part Four (Dublin, 1906), p. 6.
10. Wauchope, *Williamite War*, p. 9.
11. Ball, *A History*, p. 6.
12. ibid.
13. Sarsfield /Vesey Papers (National Archives of Ireland 2/466/2 Exchequer Documents, no. 58).
14. There was some question regarding her paternity. (www.leigh.org/genealogy/biographies/lucywalter.htm), viewed 9 December 2007.
15. The equivalent in 2007 of approx. £16,000/€25,000.
16. Wauchope, *Williamite War*, p. 9.
17. ibid., p. 27.
18. ibid., p. 8.
19. Lady Honora's second marriage was to James FitzJames, duke of Berwick on Tweed, natural son of James II, fellow officer of her first husband.
20. Wauchope, *Williamite War* p. 89.
21. D'Alton, *Illustrations*, p. 136.
22. ibid., p. 135.
23. Piers Wauchope, 'Patrick Sarsfield, Jacobite first earl of Lucan' in H.C.G. Matthew & Brian Harrison (eds), *Dictionary of National Biography from the earliest times to 2000*, vol. xlviii, (Oxford, 2000), p. 996.
24. D'Alton, *Illustrations* p. 134.
25. Sarsfield/Vesey Papers (NAI D3474 A).
26. Ball, *A History*, p. 8.

27. H.S. Sweetman (ed.), *Calendar of Documents relating to Ireland* (London, 1881), no. 481, Close, 26 Edward I, m 9-8 dors., 22/1/1297.
28. Ball, *A History*, p. 8.
29. Sarsfield/Vesey Papers (NAI T3738)
30. ibid., (NAI D3474 A).
31. Anthony Malcomson, *de Veci Papers, Summary*, Public Record Office of Northern Ireland (1998).
32. ibid.
33. Ball, *A History*, p. 8.
34. Sarsfield/Vesey Papers (NAI D3486 B); D'Alton, *Illustrations*, p. 139.
35. Ball, *A History*, p. 9.
36. Desmond Guinness, *Lucan House* (Dublin, 2005) p. 30.
37. Ball, *A History*, p. 10.
38. Mark Bence-Jones, *A Guide to Irish Country Houses* (Dublin, 1988, reprinted 1996) p. 195.
39. ibid.
40. I am grateful to John Redmill, who has delved into the architectural history of the house, for briefly discussing this portion of the project with me and offering advice.
41. Conor Lucey, *The Stapleton collection: designs for the Irish neoclassical interior* (Tralee, 2007), p. 47-50.
42. Bence-Jones, *A Guide*. What this method comprised of is not known.
43. Arthur Young, *A Tour in Ireland* (1776-1779) Vol. I, Arthur W. Hutton (ed.), (London, 1892), p. 30.
44. Sidney Lee, 'Elizabeth Vesey', *Dictionary of National Biography*, vol. lvii (1899).
45. Guinness, *Lucan House*, p. 30; Also in conversation with John Redmill.
46. Barbara B. Schnorrenberg, 'Elizabeth Vesey c.1715-1791' in H.C.G. Matthew & Brian Harrison, (eds), *Oxford Dictionary of National Biography*, vol. lvi (Oxford, 2000), pp 390-01. Her niece would also marry into the same family see Anthony Malcomson, *Pursuit of the Heiress* (Belfast, 2006), p. 132.
47. Sir Thomas Vesey, first Baronet (1672/3-1730) bishop of Ossory (1714-30).
48. Anna Meigon, 'Biographical Sketches of Principal Bluestocking Women' in Nicole Pohl & Betty Schellenberg (eds) *Reconsidering the Bluestockings* (San Merino, 2003), p. 36.
49. Ball, *A History*, p. 9.
50. ibid.
51. Francis Elrington Ball (1863-1928), a historian whose book about County Dublin was published in 1906.
52. Schnorrenberg, *Dictionary*, p. 390.
53. Bluestocking: a name for those gathering for serious conversation rather than frivolous pursuits such as card playing and gossip. The name was coined when guest complained he did not have suitably fashionable attire to attend a meeting and was instructed to come in his blue stockings. A version of this story in Rosemary Baird, *Mistress of the house great ladies and grand houses* 1670-1830 (London 2003), p. 169.

54. Pohl & Schellenberg, *Reconsidering the Bluestockings*, p. 11.
55. Angelique Day (ed.), Letters from Georgian Ireland (Belfast, 1991), p. 279.
56. Pohl & Schellenberg, *Reconsidering the bluestockings*, p. 37.
57. Stella Tillyard, *A royal affair George III and his scandalous siblings*, (London, 2006), p. 17.
58. Amanda Vickery, *The gentleman's daughter, women's lives in Georgian England*, (London, 1998), p. 9.
59. Pohl & Schellenberg, *Reconsidering the bluestockings*, p. 6.
60. ibid.
61. Sylvia Harcstack Myers, *Bluestocking circle women friendship and the life of the mind in eighteenth-century England* (Oxford, 1990), p. 121, 123.
62. ibid., p. 125.
63. Ball, *A History*, p. 9.
64. Lady Llanover (ed.) *Mrs Delany at court and among the wits, being the record of a great lady of genius in the art of living* (London, 1925), p. 165.
65. ibid., pp 185-6.
66. ibid., p. 172.
67. Day, *Letters*, p. 104.
68. ibid., p. 105.
69. ibid., p. 167.
70. ibid., p. 109.
71. ibid.
72. ibid.
73. Ruth Hayden, *Mrs Delany her life and her flowers* (London, 1980, reprint, 2005), p. 125.
74. Professor Deborah Heller, with funding from the Huntington Library, is presently editing Elizabeth Vesey's letters for publication.
75. Brian FitzGerald, *Lady Louisa Conolly*, (London, 1950) p. 33, 37.
76. Deborah Heller, 'Subjectivity unbound: Elizabeth Vesey as the Sylph in Bluestocking correspondence' in Pohl & Schellenberg, *Reconsidering the Bluestockings*, pp 215-234.
77. FitzGerald, *Lady Louisa*, pp 33, 37.
78. Schnorrenberg, *Dictionary*, p. 390-1.
79. Agmondisham (sr) and Lady Jane Butler's daughter Catherine married Mr Anthony Jephson of Mallow, Co. Cork.
80. For a detailed discussion of inheritance practices see Anthony Malcomson, *The pursuit of the heiress* (Belfast, 2006).
81. Register of births, deaths and marriages St Mary's' Leixlip, 1778-1875, and marriage register of St Andrew's, Lucan, 1845-1950, Parish of Leixlip Union, Representative Church Body Library.
82. Mary Mulhall, *A History of Lucan* (Naas, 1991), p. 14.
83. The author wishes to thank Mary Mulhall for pointing out this memorial.
84. References to this daughter cannot, at present, be found in the Dublin repositories of births deaths and marriages.
85. De Vesci Papers (National Library of Ireland MS 39,257/6) It has not been possible

to establish at present who was Mary Cecelia Hatch.

86. The 1894 Hong Kong Plague Medal, *The Medals Year Book* (London, 1995). (http://www.lightinfantry.org.uk/Regiments/ksli/shrop_hongkong.htm), viewed March 2007.
87. De Vesci Papers (NLI MS 39, 256/5).
88. ibid.
89. ibid., (NLI MS 39,257/6).
90. Information supplied by the Colthurst family of Blarney, County Cork.
91. De Vesci Papers (NLI MS 39,266).
92. Colthurst Estate, Co. Dublin, 14 July 1925 (NLI M 1814).
93. According to Mr Rodney Cromer, whose family had owned the property, the cottage orné burnt down in 1953.
94. It is thought that the present plaster work is by Michael Stapleton (1770-1803).
95. Colthurst Estate, (M1814).
96. Toby Barnard, *A guide to Sources for the history of material culture in Ireland, 1500-2000* (Dublin 2005), pp 12-13.
97. For further discussion of material culture see Toby Barnard, *Making the grand figure, lives and possessions in Ireland* 1641-1770 (London, 2004).
98. 'A catalogue of the furniture, oil paintings, pastel portraits, old silver and plated ware china etc. at Lucan House, Lucan Co Dublin, Messers Bennett and Son will sell by auction in the above mansion Tuesday 29th September 1925': This copy with notes was kindly provided by Sir Charles St John Jefferies Colthurst of Blarney Castle and Demesne, Co. Cork.
99. Ann Finer and George Savage (eds.), *The selected letters of Josiah Wedgwood* (London, 1965), p.93.
100. De Vesci Papers (NAI MS 39,266).
101. ibid., the full rent was £1,176.
102. Web site: http://en.wikipedia.org/wiki/o'conor_don, viewed 10 September 2007.
103. Bence-Jones, *Irish Country Houses*, p. 195.
104. Sir Luke William Burke Teeling, (1903 South Dublin-1975), British MP 1944-69
105. John Constable, A series of lectures to the Royal Institution 1836, *Oxford dictionary of quotations*, (2nd ed, London, 1981), p. 77.
106. Mike Crang, *Cultural Geography* (London,1999), p. 32-33.
107. Denis E. Cosgrove, *Social formation and symbolic landscape* (London, 1998), p. 227.
108. Desmond Guinness and William Ryan, *Houses and Castles of Ireland* (London, 1971), p. 135; This bridge was 'carried away' in 1786, Ball, A *History*, p. 11.
109. Edward Malins, 'Mrs Delany and landscaping in Ireland' *Irish Georgian Society* vol. xi, nos 2 & 3, 1968, pp 1-16.
110. Katherine Conolly, widow of Speaker Conolly. Following her death Mrs Delany wrote, 'We have lost our great friend Mrs Conolly' in Guinness, *Irish Houses and Castles*, p. 200.
111. I am grateful to Deborah Heller for permission to include this quote from

Elizabeth's Veseys unpublished letters.

112. Finola O'Kane, *Landscape design in eighteenth century Ireland, mixing foreign trees with the natives* (Cork, 2004), p.168.
113. Patrick J. Duffy, *Exploring the history and heritage of Irish landscape* (Dublin, 2007), p 42.
114. Ball, *A History*, p. 53.
115. F. H. A Aalen, Kevin Whelan and Matthew Stout, (eds), *Atlas of the rural Irish landscape* (Dublin, 1997), p. 197.
116. See Mary Mulhall and Joan O'Flynn (eds), *Treasures of Lucan* (Lucan, 2007), pp 1-2.
117. This tunnel was destroyed by the building of the dual carriageway in the 1990s.
118. For a more in depth discussion of St Catherine's see *Aspects of Leixlip* (Dublin, 2001).
119. Aalen et al, *Atlas of Irish rural landscape*, p.198.
120. Registry of Deeds, 1786, Book 370, page 520, memorial 253244.
121. Stephen Daniels, 'The Iconography of Woodland' in Denis Cosgrove and Stephen Daniels (eds) *The Iconography of Landscape* (Cambridge, 1988) (this edition 2000), p. 44.
122. ibid.
123. W.J. Smyth, 'The greening of Ireland- tenant tree planting in the eighteenth and nineteenth centuries' in *Irish Forestry* no. 54 vol. I (1997), p 59.
124. Daniels, *Landscape*, p. 48.
125. ibid., p. 50.
126. ibid., p. 45.
127. Smyth, *Irish Forestry* p. 58.
128. ibid., p. 65.
129. This gate lodge is presently a private home.